Norse Mythology

A Complete Guide to Norse Mythology,

Norse Gods, and Nordic Folklore

Andrew Walsh

Table of Contents

Introduction

Congratulations on picking up *Norse Mythology*! Thank you for choosing this book.

Throughout the following chapters will discuss everything there is to know about Norse mythology, from the gods and monsters to the heroic tales that we know today. Norse mythology is rather interesting, as much of what we know has been pieced together from artifacts and poems that were completed after Christianity took over as the primary religion.

As you will learn, there were two main tribes or families of gods, the Aesir and the Vanir; each played a slightly different role in the hierarchy of Norse mythology. They had an incredible war that brought the two families together.

You will also learn about who Odin, Thor, and Loki were, and how they interacted with each other. We will take a look at some of the craziest monsters the gods ever had to face, and who may have created them.

Also, you will discover who the heroes of the Norse were, what they did to receive the title of hero, and how they were able to stand in such high esteem.

Finally, we'll take a look at some of the more interesting stories that came from this time. How was Thor's hammer, the great Mjolnir, really created? Why did Odin lose one of his eyes? How was the world created according to the Norse religion? All of these things and more will be revealed in the following chapters!

Once again, thank you for choosing this book over the numerous others on this same subject. Careful consideration was taken to include only the most accurate information in this book. Please enjoy!

Chapter 1: The Origins of Norse Mythology

The first known mentions of Norse mythology were during the time of the Vikings (790 to 1100 CE), and it was a vibrant and thriving religion. The Scandinavian people believed in the god Odin, who had only one eye, and created the numerous other gods and goddesses within their religion. Many grand tales came from this religion, including stories detailing the creation of earth and the eventual destruction of earth.

Though this was a religion, most people simply considered it to be a tradition, and it was a guiding factor in their lives. Eventually, Christianity took over the region, and their religion was all but wiped out.

Finding the Lost Religion

Due to Christianity taking over, it has been difficult to piece together what had once been Norse Mythology. The parts that are known in the modern age come from poetry, both Eddic and Skaldic poetry. The Eddic poetry was from *Poetic Edda*, which was first compiled around 1270 CE, but more than likely originated before the 10th century, which was when Christianity began to take over. Skaldic poetry was directly from the Viking age and was often recited by kings at court.

These poems were often not of complete tales, as it was assumed the audience already knew the tales they spoke of. In the *Poetic Edda*, there was a *Codex Regius* that documented twenty-nine older poems, nineteen about Norse heroes and ten about Norse gods. These were beneficial at giving an insight into the gods and tales of the Norse religion.

Medieval sources from about 1220 CE, like *Prose Edda*, written by Snorri Sturluson, were reworked tales from Viking origins. Though they were written within a Christian context, they provided a more cohesive and finished story.

Some of what modern-day scholars know of Norse mythology also comes from legends in Scandinavian folklore, or what has survived of it. These tales appeared in other Germanic literature, like the Anglo-Saxon Battle of Finnsburgh, which has similarities to Deor mythological tales.

Many runestones have references to the myths found in poems and other places. Hyrrokkin riding to Baldr's funeral was referenced in one of the Hunnestad Monument stones that has survived. Other stones have depictions of Odin being eaten by Fenrir, and of Sigurd the dragon slayer. All of these combined have given us a better idea of what Norse mythology truly was.

Religion in Viking Society

As stated earlier, the Viking people did not consider this a religion. It was simply a tradition or custom they followed that helped guide their lives. There is a lot of archaeological evidence that suggests there were many who had a personal devotion to a specific god or gods. These people also conducted daily rituals to confirm their devotion.

Many of these rituals also point to the Norse gods having their own unique personalities. This was different from other ancient religions, where the gods ruled over some specific aspect of life, like fertility or the trees.

Often, gods were worshiped. Certain places, like Fröslunda, were given names that were directly related to the name of a god. Fröslunda translates to "the grove dedicated to the god Freyr" who is one of the Vanir gods.

Every nine years, people would gather at a great temple in Uppsala, which is located in Sweden, to offer sacrifice to Thor, Odin, and Freyr. These sacrifices were completed during times of disease, war, famine, or weddings and were often done using humans, dogs, and horses. There is no archeological evidence to support the idea of a temple, but there are many buildings and great halls that were uncovered in this area.

The myths that accompany this religion are vast and begin right at the creation of the world. The myths then continue all the way through to the destruction of the world during Ragnarök, and then through to the rising of the new world.

Most scholars agree that Norse mythology was not a stagnant religion that did not change. It would change based on local beliefs and through time, especially when Christianity came into play. At first, they added Christ and the beliefs that accompanied Him to their religion, side by side, with their other gods. Over time, their polytheistic views became monotheistic, with Christianity at the helm.

Difference Between Aesir and Vanir Families

Though these two families both resided in Asgard, which was the home of the gods, they had different ideas on how to do things. The Aesir were most known for advising kings on war, and also on how to govern their people. The Vanir were best known for their fertility, good weather, and farming.

Evidence of this was seen in who the Viking people worshipped. Those who were in positions of power were more likely to be seen worshipping the Aesir gods, looking to them for guidance on how to accomplish their latest task. Farmers, on the other hand, were much more interested in following the practices of the Vanir gods.

Due to this, some believe different families were created as a direct result of the differences between these people. This way, each would have their gods to help them through the most difficult of times.

In Norse mythology, these two families were at two opposing ends. Each did not like the way the other governed, and this eventually led to a giant war, called either the Vanir war, or the Aesir-Vanir war. Neither side truly won, but they did declare peace.

With this peace, they traded some of their people and had those people married within, combining their families into one.

Chapter 2: The Aesir Gods and Goddesses

The most popular Norse gods belong to the Aesir family. These gods have been portrayed numerous times in popular culture, both in movies and books, and have some of the most interesting stories.

Everyone in the Aesir tribe lived in Asgard, which was one of the Nine Worlds. Asgard was located on the sunniest and highest branch of the Yggdrasil world-tree. As such, they often considered Asgard as the best of the Nine Worlds.

The Yggdrasil tree is most commonly referred to as an ash tree, though there is no set idea of what type of tree it is. It is called the Yggdrasil tree as an homage to Odin, as it roughly translates to the "Horse of Odin." This name refers to one of the many tales in Norse mythology, where Odin, who was also called 'the Terrible One', sacrificed himself to discover runes.

The Gods

The Aesir tribe was home to at least twenty-five different gods, which were the principal gods in Norse mythology. More than anything, the gods in the Aesir tribe stood for war, which is why many of them are very powerful. Among them, one was the chief of the Aesir tribe, Odin.

Odin

As the leader of the Aesir tribe, Odin has many stories and tales written about him. He prides himself on giving wisdom to others, but does not hold much importance in justice or law. He is one of the most contradictory gods in Norse mythology, but also one of the most important.

One translation of his name is "Master of Ecstasy," coming from the Old Norse name of Óôinn. Another translation, which came in the eleventh century, is "The Furious," which is quite appropriate in many tales of Odin. The second translation is most noted during times of war in the tales of Odin, as he was considered terrifying when mad.

To the Norse people, he was not the incredibly honorable ruler that he is seen as today. In fact, he was often seen as an inciter of peaceful people, driving them towards war. The Norse people also believed he enjoyed forcing people to go to war.

Though Odin was one of the driving forces behind most wars, he never wanted to associate himself with the average person. If he did associate himself, it was only with the warrior who held the most power. The Volsung family, considered to be one of the great Germanic heroes, were one of the few who held Odin's patronage.

Warrior-shamans or berserkers also held high favor with Odin. They used fighting techniques associated with ferocious animals like wolves and bears. They also conducted spiritual practices behind these animals, and since Odin was the master of these animals, they closely associated themselves with him.

Odin is the founder of many of the royal lines in Norse mythology. Many of these kings turned to Odin to be their beneficiary. The Germanic people had a three-tiered hierarchy within their society, much like other peoples of that time. The first tier was made of rulers, the second tier was made of warriors, and the third tier was made of the people associated with producing something, like farmers. Above all, Odin was always associated with the first tier.

Generally, he liked to rule with magic and cunning and was often seen as the devious ruler. Though he was most regularly associated with kings, he also associated himself with outlaws, helping them succeed in their various escapades. These people were no longer part of society as they had been banished for crimes they had committed. Like Odin, they did not care about established laws, which only made Odin someone they wanted to follow even more.

A Danish historian in the late twelfth and early thirteenth centuries spoke of a tale where Odin had been banished from Asgard for ten years because of how bad his reputation had become. This effort was to save the reputation of other gods and goddesses in Asgard from being tarnished.

Odin saw limitations as something to overcome. He always strived to have more wisdom, power, and knowledge and would gain these by any means necessary. For the most part, these means were magical.

One of the most interesting features of Odin is his single eye. He sacrificed the other in an effort to gain more wisdom, which is one of the most famous tales in Norse mythology.

In another effort to gain more wisdom, he hung himself from Yggdrasil, the world tree, for nine days. He forbid anyone from giving him any food or water. By the end of the nine days, he was able to see the hidden runes, which detailed a set of laws for the Norse people to follow.

An interesting aspect of Odin is his ability to speak only in poetry. Originally, he had stolen the mead of poetry from the giants. This was the source of how to speak and write the most beautiful poetry. He would grant the gift of poetry using the mead only to those he believed were worthy.

In terms of the dead, Odin is the one who presides over Valhalla. Valhalla is the best dwelling-place for the dead. After any battle was waged, Odin and the Valkyries would choose half of the dead to bring back to Valhalla, leaving the other half for Freya from the Venir tribe.

He was often the receiver of human sacrifices, most often of royalty. These sacrifices were usually made with a spear, noose, or occasionally using both. This was the same way Odin had hung himself from the Yggdrasil tree. During a battle, someone might throw a spear at their foes and shout, "Odin owns ye all" to draw favor from Odin to help them in battle.

One of his most popular titles is that of "Allfather" as he is considered both an Aesir god and a Vanir god, while also being part giant, as his mother was one of the first frost giants. The god Odr from the Vanir tribe is considered an extension of Odin himself. He was one of the biggest parts of the creation of the world, which never could have happened without his influence.

Thor

As the God of Thunder, Thor is one of the most prominent gods in Norse mythology. Thor was considered a major god in all branches of the Norse people from the beginning right up until they converted to Christianity. By far, he was most popular during the late Viking Age among the Scandinavian people.

He is the perfect archetype of a warrior who shows both loyalty and honor, something a human warrior aspired to possess. Thor is most often depicted protecting Asgard from the giants, who were often their enemy. He was also the biggest defender of the Aesir gods, using his power over thunder to keep his people safe.

Thor is one of Odin's sons, with his mother being a giantess named Jörd. Thor had a wife named Sif, though little is known about her except that the dwarves handcrafted her golden hair after Loki shaved her head. He had one daughter with Sif named Thrud, two sons with his giantess mistress Járnsaxa named Modi and Magni, and had a stepson named Ull, who was the son of Sif.

He wielded the iconic Mjolnir, a war hammer that would magically return to the user after being thrown. This hammer also had the ability to shoot thunder. To carry the hammer, he wore a belt called Megingjord to boost his strength, and special iron gloves to lift the hammer, as it was much too heavy for the average person to hold. Together, using all of these items, he was best prepared to kill giants, which was his primary duty.

In many tales, he can be seen riding in a chariot pulled by goats, whose names translate to Tooth-Grinder and Tooth-Gnasher. One of the *Prose Edda* stories states that whenever he was hungry, he could kill and roast the goats, but then touch the remains of the goats with his hammer to bring them back to life once again.

The cult of Thor was one of the largest cults in Norse mythology. He had an incredibly active group of priests who worshipped him throughout the Scandanavian world. Even as they began to transition into Christianity, many people drew comparisons between Thor's power and the power of Christ. This is mostly shown in poems that survived, where Thor is addressed using only second-person pronouns, and is thanked for defending the world against chaos.

In Germany, there was a sacred tree called Thor's Oak, which had been one of the most prominent religious sights for Norse mythology. However, Saint Boniface decided to cut the tree down in 723 to show the superiority of the Christian God over the Nordic gods.

Though Thor had strong ties with the protection of Asgard, he also had some association with fertility and agriculture. In particular, his control of thunder and air could bring rains to farmlands to keep them prosperous.

There are numerous tales about his physical prowess, many of which are connected with him killing monsters and giants, especially those monsters that were creations of Loki. Midgard, the land of the humans, had many monsters that Loki had unleashed upon it, such as the Midgard serpent.

Even with his immense power, Thor was eventually defeated by the Midgard serpent, who spat venom at him. After his death, his sons Modi and Magni took over control of Mjolnir.

Loki

Loki is the god of mischief, lies, and tricks, and tended to create monsters to attack the people of Asgard. He is always depicted as a conniving coward who cares more about self-preservation and playing tricks than anything else. Even when he appeared to be helpful, there was a good chance he would turn and stab those that he had helped in the back.

He is the child of at least one giant, his father, Farbauti. His mother, Laufey, may have been a giant, but some stories suggest that she may have been a goddess, or something else completely.

He is the parent of many different species, some being animals and some being gods like him. One of his children, Hel, is the goddess of the underworld, who was conceived with the giantess Angrboda. He also had Jormungand, the Midgard serpent who killed Thor during Ragnarok, and Fenrir, a wolf who killed Odin during Ragnarok, with this giantess. He also had a son named either Nari or Narfi with his wife, Sigyn. Finally, he transformed himself into a mare and became impregnated by a stallion Svadilfari, giving birth to Sleipnir, which was Odin's shamanic horse.

Even though Loki is one of the Aesir gods, he shows no concern for any of them. This is especially evident in the number of gods he sent his children to kill and attack. There is a poem that describes how Loki went to the hall of the Aesir and proceeded to defame and mock the gods and goddesses who were present.

He also was often seen helping the gods fix issues he had created in the first place. For example, when he sheared Sif's hair, he then decided to help them create a wig to replace it. Along with this, there were times he outright helped the gods by tricking others for their benefit. One example was when he tricked a giant who aided them by building walls around Asgard without being paid.

Even though he does occasionally assist the gods, most of the dislike for Loki comes from his role in killing Baldur, which caused Ragnarok; something you will learn more about later.

Interestingly enough, even though he is mentioned in many tales, there is little to no mention of him outside of the northernmost Germanic countries. This made historians believe he may have been a regional god rather than a god throughout all of Norse mythology. There is also no evidence that he had a cult, which makes it even more probable he was worshipped regionally.

Frigg

As the highest-ranking goddess within the Aesir tribe, Frigg was Odin's wife and Baldur's mother. Even though she held such a high position of power, the majority of sources on her do not only speak of her, but also of Freya. Freya was a goddess within the Venir and Aesir tribes. Nearly all of their stories and traits are identical except for their name.

Frigg used the power of seidr, which was Norse magic, to bring about change to the world. This was done by creating new events and changing the course of the future. Those who had this power were called völva.

Like many other gods and goddesses from this time, she was not always in a position where people loved her. There were times where she was feared and scorned, and other times when she was celebrated.

One way historians have tried to differentiate between Frigg and Freya is based on their promiscuity. There are tales where they both slept with others outside of their marriage, but historians like to say that Freya slept around with many more people than Frigg did. However, there are tales of Frigg sleeping with Odin's brothers regularly while he was exiled from Asgard.

One interesting fact about Frigg is the word "Friday." This word originated from Frija, the goddess who is believed to be the original before Frigg and Freya were born. Therefore, the word Friday is directly derived from both Frigg and Freya.

Baldur

Baldur was one of the most beloved gods in Norse mythology. He was handsome and cheerful, and his body gave off light. He was so loved that when he began to have dreams of his death, his mother visited everything in the world and made it swear not to harm him.

He was the son of Odin and Frigg, and had one full brother, Hodr. He also had many half-brothers from Odin, like Thor, Heimdall, and Bragi, and a half-brother who was conceived after his death named Vali as a way to avenge his death. He was married to Nanna, a goddess, and they had a son named Forseti, who was associated with justice and peace.

During his life, he had a large ship called Hringhorni that was said to be the greatest ship ever to be built. His body was placed in this ship after his death as a funeral pyre and sent downriver. He also had a horse named Lettfeti that was eventually sacrificed on his funeral pyre.

By far, the story of his death was his most remarkable tale. He was rarely mentioned outside of this tale, only in a few pre-Christianity stories. When he was mentioned, it was about his splendor and how he held such a high place in the hearts and minds of the Viking people.

Heimdall

Above all else, Heimdall was a protector of those who came and went from the Nine Worlds. He was said to have keen hearing and sight, making him the perfect guardian of the gods. He was seen as a father and patron to the humans living in Midgard because of his strong role in granting wisdom.

Interestingly, Heimdall was often associated with things like the sea, gold, roosters, and rams, which came from his mothers. It was said he had nine mothers who were sea giants, named Gjolp, Atla, Greip, Ulfrun, Jarnsaxa, Eistla, Angeyja, Eyrgjafa, and Imth. This was most likely a reference to his guardianship over the nine worlds.

In the *Prose Edda*, it was said he required very little sleep, even less than a bird would, that he could see perfectly in the dark, and that he could spot an enemy from a hundred leagues away. Also noted was his sense of hearing, which was so powerful he could hear as the grass grew, and wool grew on sheep.

The one object he held dear was his horn, called Gjallarhorn. This horn was said to be the loudest horn one could blow. In fact, according to the legends, when he realized Ragnarok was coming, he was able to blow this horn to signal to all the gods they needed to return for the battle.

Unlike other gods, he never got married. Instead, he focused on reproducing with humans, all of which remained nameless. However, these humans were said to be the original creators of three different human classes.

Tyr

Tyr was the god of war in Norse mythology. He was considered an incredible warrior who fought for justice and order. At some point, he engaged in a fight with Fenrir, the wolf child of Loki, and lost part of his right arm.

Two people could have potentially been his father. One was Hymir, who was a giant mentioned in a section of the *Poetic*

Edda. The other was Odin, who seemed to have fathered many of the greatest Norse gods. Most scholars agree that his father was most likely Odin.

There is no mention of who his mother was, but the section of the *Poetic Edda* called *Hymiskvitha* did mention his grandmother had not one head, but nine hundred heads instead.

Outside of his incredible warrior skills, he was also blessed with incredible wisdom, which aided him in battle and his fight for justice. While he was not mentioned in many myths, the two he was prominent in were *Hymiskvitha* and *Ragnarok.*

His name is also said to be the origin of the day Tuesday, which was initially meant to signify "Tyr's Day." Romans associated him with Mars, which was the war god they believed in.

Idun

She was a goddess who was best known for the tale 'The Kidnapping of Idun', which is one of the most well-known tales from this period. Her role in this tale was that of the owner and provider of immortality-giving fruit, which is most believed to be apples.

Due to this incredible fruit, her role in Asgard was immense. She was the reason the gods were able to stay young, as she provided them fruit whenever they began to feel the effects of aging.

Her husband was Bragi, who was Asgard's prime court minstrel and poet. In one poem, Loki accuses her of sleeping with her brother's murderer, but no evidence could back this accusation up. There are no known names associated with who her brother or her brother's murderer were.

There is not much known about Idun, but there are still references to her in modern-day pop culture. Generally, these references depict her magical immortality-giving fruit more than anything else.

Bragi

Most mythology regarding Bragi is focused on his poetry, especially when he regales the Einherjar, who are the dead who dwell in Valhalla. He also welcomed the newly dead heroes into their midst.

In one interpretation, Bragi was not a god at first. He was the historical bard named Bragi Boddason, whose poems were incredible and artful. Because of his wild success, he was granted a spot as the court poet in Valhalla by Odin after his death.

Under that interpretation, he was not considered a god until the Old Norse writers of the Middle Ages elevated him to the level of a god.

However, in other interpretations, he was the son of Odin and was married to Idun. Here, he was considered the god of poetry and music and was incredibly wise, just like other Norse gods. Bragi Boddason was still known as a famous poet, but he was not the Bragi who was worshipped as the god of poetry.

His most distinctive features were his incredibly long beard, and the runes that were carved onto his tongue.

Vili and Ve

As two brothers of Odin, they were directly related to the creation of the cosmos, the beginning of all things in Norse mythology. They also slept with Frigg while Odin was exiled from Asgard. Not much else is known about them, but there are a few times they pop up in various Norse tales.

Though their contributions seem to be small, they were likely worshipped heavily by the Germanic tribes during the Viking Age. Since they were the brothers of Odin, who was the Allfather of the gods, they would have held some sort of important status.

Forseti

There is not much known about the god Forseti. What is known is that he is the god of justice and the son of Baldur and Nanna. He is considered one of the twelve leading gods, but was not a significant figure in any of the myths that have survived.

His dwelling place was in a courthouse called Glitnir, which glittered of silver and gold. It was there that he settled any disputes by acting as a divine judge. This was his primary role in Norse mythology.

Gefjun

She was the goddess of fertility, abundance, agriculture, and prosperity. Most of what modern-day scholars know of her comes from the historian Snorri Sturluson from the thirteenth century.

It was said that she disguised herself as a beggar woman and went to the king of Sweden, Gylfi. There, she asked him if he could give her land. He granted her whatever land she could plow in a single day and night. Of course, she immediately got to work and had her four sons, who were oxes, plow the land. This plowing went so deep into the land that it created an entire island, which is now known as part of Denmark called Zealand.

There are some similarities between Gefjun and the goddess Freya. They were both earth goddesses who delivered peace and bountiful fields, and they were both accused by Loki to have exchanged sex for jewels. They may be the same god, although many Norse gods were similar, yet separate.

Sif

This goddess was mostly mentioned in passing throughout the many tales that have survived. She was Thor's wife and had one son with someone who was not Thor, Ullr. The biggest tale associated with her was when Loki cut off her golden hair, which was part of The Creation of Thor's Hammer.

Many scholars note that her golden hair could be symbolic of the golden fields of grain when they were ready for harvesting. As Thor was often associated with agriculture, it is a fairly easy assumption to make.

Also associated with Thor's agricultural prowess, it could be said that Sif was one of the many goddesses that were associated with bountiful harvests and fertility of the earth. There is also a species of moss that was called haddr Siffar, which seems to be a direct link to Sif herself.

Other Gods

There were other gods of the Aesir tribe who were less well-known and were occasionally giants. These gods had very little prevalence in the surviving tales, but they are still worth mentioning for their contributions.

Fjorgynn and Fjorgyn

These two are male and female. They were giants who did not have any significant roles in the surviving tales but were mentioned in passing. Fjorgyn, the female, was said to be the mother of Thor, though there is also a possibility his mother was Jord. Many references suggest that Fjorgyn and Jord were the same giantess.

As for Fjorgynn, there was a reference to him in the Poetic Edda, where Frigg was called Fjorgynn's moer, which translates to "Fjorgynn's maiden." That could either mean she was his mistress or his daughter. Most believe she was his mistress.

Jord

Jord was one of the other names given to Thor's mother, though not the only one. All of the names written in the poetry referencing Thor's mother all mean earth, which means it is possible all of these names mentioned were of the same person.

Sol and Mani

Their names directly translate to Sun (Sol) and Moon (Mani), which suggests they were the gods of the sun and moon, respectively. They were brother and sister, Sol being the sister and Mani being the brother. After the world was created, the other gods created the concept of day and night, different parts of the year, and phases of the moon so they both knew what to do.

Both of them ride on horse-drawn chariots through the sky, completing their daily cycles. They have to ride quickly through the sky as there are two wolves, Skoll and Hati, who eventually overtake them during Ragnarok.

Ullr

He is the son of Sif and stepson of Thor. The knowledge modern-day scholars do have of him states that he was a significant figure, though they have little idea why that may have been as there are very few passing references.

He was incredibly skilled at skiing, skating, archery, and hunting. Ullr was often called upon by the Norse people before engaging in a duel. Numerous places throughout Sweden and Norway have the name Ullr in the names, which only further proves he was an important figure at one time.

Hoenir

Hoenir is another god there is little known about. Hoenir does play a role in one of the poems from the Poetic Edda, the *Voluspa*. Here, he was a part of the creation of the first humans along with Odin and Loourr, who was another god there is little information about.

There are a few other mentions of him, but they are limited to being a travel companion to Odin and Loki. One historian, Kennings, described him with long legs and as swift. He was also referred to as the most fearful out of all the gods. Through all of these interpretations, there is not a single, solid version of who he was as a god.

Vidar

Vidar was a God who was only mentioned for his role in Ragnarok and nothing else. Due to this, little is truly known about his personality or what he did outside of this instance. In some tellings of Ragnarok, he was one of the few survivors.

He was a son of Odin, who decided to try to avenge his father's death at the hands of Fenrir. As he had shoes specifically designed with sturdiness and magic, he was able to kick Fenrir's lower jaw open, hold it open with his hand, and kill him.

There is one other mention of him where he is called the silent god, and no explanation is given about why that is.

Hodr

Hodr is mostly associated with a single tale in Norse mythology, where he played a rather large role. In the death of Baldur, he was the one who was tricked by Loki into using a mistletoe spear to kill Baldur. As he was blind and very gullible, he had not understood what he was doing until after.

There is, however, another version of this tale that is wildly different. In this other version, Hodr and Baldur were war leaders who were trying to win Nanna's hand in marriage. Baldur was incredibly strong, and Hodr knew he would not be able to defeat him easily. He then traveled to the underworld, got a spear that was magically infused, and used it to wound Baldur, who eventually succumbed to his wounds.

Vali

Vali is most well known as the god who avenged the death of Baldur by killing Hodr. He killed Hodr when he was only one day old, which suggests that he may have been explicitly born to avenge Baldur. He is also mentioned as one of the few who survived Ragnarok.

Sigyn

The little known about Sigyn was that she was the wife of Loki and had a single son with him, whose name was either Narfi, or Nari. She was mentioned in passing during the tale that explained Loki's punishment for assisting in killing Baldur. There, the other gods turned one of his other sons named Vali (different from the Vali who avenged Baldur's death) into a wolf to kill Narfi/Nari.

The gods used the entrails of Narfi/Nari to bind Loki and have a snake drip venom onto his head. Sigyn held a bowl above his head to catch the venom from the snake to keep him from feeling pain. Of course, when she did need to empty the bowl, Loki's agony from the venom created intense earthquakes on earth.

Chapter 3: The Vanir Gods and Goddesses

The Vanir gods are the other principal tribe in Norse mythology. Before they joined with the Aesir gods in Asgard, they lived in Vanaheim, which is one of the Nine Worlds. There were significantly fewer Vanir gods than Aesir gods, only six of which played a significant role in Norse mythology.

Though these two tribes, the Aesir and Vanir, are part of the same mythology, they often had squabbles and did not see eye to eye on many things. They did eventually come together and marry within each other's families, but it took a war to happen before they saw eye to eye on anything.

The Gods

The Vanir gods are often associated with fertility moreso than the war that the Aesir gods are mostly associated with. Arguably, the most famous Vanir goddess is Freya, who is often associated with the Aesir goddess Frigg.

Freya

Freya is one of the biggest names in the Vanir family. She is the goddess of fertility who had an immense love for both material possessions, and her beauty. Often, she is depicted as someone who slept around with anyone she could. She loved having fun, particularly in the form of parties.

She had a brother named Freyr, who was also a god of fertility. Their father was named Njord, another fertility god, but their mother remains unknown. There was some debate that their mother could have been Nerthus, but there is no evidence to prove this is true.

She eventually married Odr, who, in many ways, is identical to Odin, which only further shows Freya and Frigg could have been the same person. They had two children together, Hnoss and Gersemi, who were both females and whose names both meant "treasure."

Her most prized possession was that of a necklace called Brisingamen. This necklace was forged by dwarves and was bought for a very high price. She guarded it very closely, never leaving it out of her sight for fear of it being stolen by thieves. She also rode a chariot that glittered and was pulled by two domestic cats.

Often, she was seen with her familiar, which is a mythical creature or animal that would assist her in magical duties, named Hildisvini. This familiar was a hog whose name translates to "battle swine."

Loki, on one occasion, actually accused her of sleeping around with every god and elf they knew, including her brother. Even with all the crazy acts of sex she is known for; there is more to her than initially meets the eye.

As with Frigg, she is known as a volva, or someone who practices the Norse magic of seidr. It was thought she was the original holder of this magic and brought it to the gods, who then showed it to the humans. With her incredible ability to control the health, desire, and prosperity of other people around her, it comes as no surprise that she was incredibly knowledgeable and powerful.

As a volva, she could bring about changes to the future by creating new events. There is one story that involves her using magic to create falcon plumes that allowed her to change her body into that of a falcon.

In an Old Norse poem, it speaks of how Freya will take half of the bodies left on a battlefield, after Odin takes his half, and bring them back to her afterlife realm of Folkyang. This realm is completely under her control, but there is nothing in the poem that states if she has any specifications to what bodies she chooses. Folkyang is not nearly as well-known as Valhalla, as there is nowhere near the number of stories written about it.

With the subtle differences in Freya and Frigg, they are just different enough where it is believed they were different gods. In the Viking Age, it is thought that they enjoyed having multiple gods who all worked to accomplish the same things, even if that made the gods themselves practically identical. In other religions, they would likely have combined the two gods rather than kept them separate.

After the end of the Aesir-Vanir war, both sides sent hostages to the other. Freya ended up being one of those hostages. From there, she became an honorary member of the Aesir tribe to keep the peace between the sides.

Freyr

Out of the Vanir gods, Freyr was the most widely worshipped god by the Norse people. He was a god of peace and prosperity, and was directly linked to fertility. More than anything, he was closely associated with good weather and male virility. No one disliked him, which was surprising considering how many other gods had different periods of dislike.

Generally, he was depicted wearing a large phallus, which was customary of fertility gods. He was most worshipped during weddings and harvest feasts, where his good fortune could rub off on those attending.

He is the brother of Freya, potentially twin brother, and the son of Njord. It is believed that their mother may have been Njord's sister Nerthus, but there is nothing to support this.

Instead of settling with one person, he was with many giantesses and goddesses. One of those potential goddesses may have been his sister, which seemed to be a common practice in the Vanir tribe.

Freyr was particularly worshiped in Sweden. He had a magical ship called Skidbladnir, which was dwarven made. It was incredibly fast and could be easily folded up to fit into a bag, or Freyr's pocket when he did not need it.

Another dwarven-made object he held dear was a mechanical boar named Gullinbursti. This boar had golden bristles and a golden mane, both of which would light the way in the darkest of places. It was able to run through both air and water faster than a horse could.

One particular object that he held was incredibly impressive. It was a sword that could fight on its own, something that was particularly important when he was in battle. However, he eventually lost this sword, which led to his death during Ragnarok.

He traveled the land using a chariot that was pulled by boars. This is likely a reflection of the historical ritual priests did, where they traveled by chariot carrying a statue of their god.

Instead of living in Vanaheim with the rest of the Vanir gods, he resided in Alfheim. Alfheim was the world of the elves. There was some speculation that he may have been the leader of the elves, but this was never explicitly said in the surviving tales. There is very little stated about the relationship between elves and gods, so it is entirely possible he was the leader of the elves in some capacity.

After the Aesir-Vanir War, Freyr was one of the gods sent to the Aesir tribe as a hostage. He then became an honorary member of the Aesir tribe.

In Ragnarok, he was destined to meet with the giant Surt. They both fought each other valiantly, but due to Freyr having lost his sword, he was defeated by Surt.

Njord

In some ways, Njord was the birth of the Vanir tribe. His children, Freya and Freyr were both incredibly well-loved gods within the Vanir family, and Freya was often regarded as the leader of the Vanir family. Njord was primarily associated with wealth, the sea, fertility, and seafaring in the ways of boats. This made him a particularly strong god to stand behind if venturing out to sea.

The Norse people had a saying when it came to the wealthy; "as rich as Njord"; as he was the god of wealth.

Njord was married to the giantess Skadi for a short time after he became an honorary member of the Aesir tribe. One Norse tale, The Marriage of Njord and Skadi, goes into detail about the marriage. She had gone to Aesir to seek restitution for her father being killed. The gods stated she could marry the god of her choice. Mistakenly, she married Njord, believing him to be Baldur.

As they lived in vastly different places, they both tried living with each other but disliked the area. Skadi lived in a snowy mountain, a place Njord despised. Meanwhile, Njord lived on the beach in Noatun, which Skadi could not stand. They ended up parting ways.

After the Aesir-Vanir war, Njord was one of the Vanir gods sent to the Aesir as a hostage. There, he became an honorary member of the Aesir tribe.

There are not many surviving stories involving Njord, even though he was one of the most worshipped gods. However, there are some accounts that many shrines and temples were created to worship him.

Nerthus

Nerthus was a rather obscure goddess who does not have many surviving accounts about her. She was most popular in some of the Germanic tribes on the European continent, but was not widely followed. From what we can gather, she was someone who was seen as Mother Earth.

Nerthus would spend her days riding on a chariot throughout the humans, helping them with their needs. Her chariot was pulled by cows, showing her strong association with nature and fertility.

The humans at the villages she stopped at would throw grand parties and rejoice at the arrival of their goddess. During those times, no one would fight, and there would be no war. Once she decided it was time to leave, however, the chariot, everything she had brought with her, and Nerthus herself would all be cleansed in a lake by slaves. These slaves would then be drowned afterward.

There is not much known about Nerthus. She is believed to be a sister of Njord and may have been the mother to Freya and Freyr, though there is little evidence to back that claim.

Gullveig

There is very little known about Gullveig. The only mention of her in the surviving poems was in two stanzas leading up to the Aesir-Vanir War. In this poem, it was evident she was practiced in the art of seidr, which is the Norse version of magic.

They speak of how she was burned numerous times in Asgard but continued to be reborn. They also speak of how she became extraordinarily powerful in the art of magic to the point where she was determined to be only for "evil women." It was believed that those who continued the study of seidr would one day become too personally powerful and would be antisocial.

Though there is no specific reference to where she came from, she is believed to be from Vanaheim. When she first came to Asgard, the magic she was performing was seen as dangerous by the Aesir people. They decided the best course of action was to burn her, which did not work as she was able to protect herself with that same magic.

Some scholars have made the connection that Gullveig may have been Freya, just with a different name. They both had a strong connection to material things and possessed strong seidr magic. However, like with many other gods, they may have just been two different gods with very similar personalities.

Odr

Though he is the husband of the goddess Freya, Odr is rarely mentioned in the surviving texts. His name means inspiration, frenzy, ecstasy, and fury. There are a lot who speculate that Odr may have been Odin, just with a different name.

Most of the time, he is mentioned; his role is passive, where he does not do anything. One example is a story where he left the other gods and went somewhere far away. There was no reasoning behind why he left or where he went to. Freya searched for him everywhere and cried golden tears because he was gone.

He had two children with Freya, Hnoss, and Gersemi. Outside of this little bit of information, not much else is known about him.

Chapter 4: The Heroes and Their Journies

Within all of the significant mythologies, there are always some people who stand out for their heroic deeds. Whether it was slaying an immense monster or protecting their people from destruction, these heroes are ones no one should ever forget. Depending on whose side of the story you're on, some of these heroes may in fact appear to be villains! All the same, they have interesting stories, and in this chapter we will share the famous tales of three such characters.

Wayland

This legend follows three brothers, Wayland, Slagfinn, and Egil, as they went out to hunt. They came to a place called Wolf Dales, which was near Wolf Lake, where they decided to build a house. One morning, they noticed three women who were sitting by the lake weaving linen. These three women were not just ordinary women but were Valkyries, which was obvious from the swan cloaks lying beside them.

Each brother married one of the Valkyries: Slagfinn with Ladgunn Swanwhite, Egil with Olrun, and Wayland with Hervor Allwise. Ladgunn and Hervor were both daughters of King Lodvi, while Olrun was the daughter of King Kiar.

They lived together for seven years before the Valkyries became restless. They longed to go back to war and left when the three brothers were away. Immediately, Slagfinn and Egil left to go find their wives and bring them home, but Wayland decided it was best to stay home to wait.

While his brothers were gone, he started a business of forging objects to sell. He created hundreds of different jewelry pieces, combining precious gems and rings to create stunning works of jewelry. However, stories of his forging reached the ears of a greedy king named Nidud. Of course, the greedy king decided he would steal the rings that Wayland had made.

Nidud led an army to Wolf Dales and took a single ring off of the line of seven hundred Wayland had made. When Wayland returned and realized one of his rings was missing, he first assumed his wife had finally returned. Comforted by the thought, he fell asleep by a fire.

When he awoke, he realized he had been shackled. Nidud told him all of the treasures he had taken to make the rings were rightfully his, but of course, Wayland disagreed. Nidud brought him back to his court, stealing anything of interest from Wayland's house, and gave the ring he had stolen to his daughter.

Nidud's queen, however, was worried. She saw nothing but drive to kill them in Wayland's eyes and warned Nidud of this fact. She stated the best thing to do would be cutting off Walyland's legs up to his knees. That way, he would be no threat. Some versions of the story say that his legs were cut off, and in others it is said that just his tendons were cut, making him lame. Either way, once he had been crippled, Wayland was sent to an island to continue forging, but solely for the King.

Sometime later, King Nidud's two sons came to the island wanting to see what kind of things Wayland had created. Seeing this as the perfect opportunity, Wayland showed them a few things before promising to give them everything he had, as long as they came back the next day in secret. Controlled by their greed, they happily came back the next day, having told no one where they were going. When Wayland opened one of the heaviest chests he had, and the two sons looked in, he let the lid fall and slice their heads clean off.

He hid their bodies but decided to craft their heads into drinking goblets for Nidud, casting them in silver. He also used their eyes in jewels created for the queen. However, his revenge did not stop there.

Bodvild, Nidud's daughter, had broken Wayland's ring, the one Nidud had stolen and given to her. She went to his island alone to keep her father from finding out what had happened. Wayland showed her a lot of kindness and she thought nothing of the drink he had given her. She became drunk quickly, and Wayland had his way with her.

Prompted by the success of killing the sons and dishonoring the daughter, he donned a feathered cape and flew to Nidud's court. When the King saw Wayland, he demanded to know what had happened.

Wayland described in great detail what he had done to all of his children, leaving nothing out. He then escaped, flying away to his freedom.

Sinfjotli

Sinfjotli is one of Sigmund's sons, and spent most of his time continuously fighting in wars. There was a time where he found a woman who he fell in love with and paid to court her. Unfortunately, his stepmother's brother had the same idea. They fought, which ended with Sinfjotli killing the brother.

His stepmother, Borghild, wanted nothing to do with him when he returned. Sinfjotli decided he would pay her in what was called wergild, where an amount was determined to compensate for death or injury.

She threw a large party in celebration of her brother. There, she filled a drinking horn with a great drink, which had been mixed with poison. She gave it to Sinfjotli, who immediately noticed there was something wrong with it. Sigmund, his father, was immune to all poisons, and so Sinfjotli gave it to him to drink. Borghild then made another drink, which Sinfjotli once again gave to Sigmund.

On the third drink, however, Borghild said he should drink it if he had the courage of the Volsungs, his family name. Sigmund was much too drunk and told him to drink it through his beard. Of course, this caused Sinfjotli to fall dead within seconds. Sigmund brought his body to a narrow fjord, where there was a man in a boat. The man offered to bring them across the water, but Sinfjotli's body had made the boat too heavy.

Sigmund had to walk around the fjord on foot until he reached the other side, but before he could even begin, the boat had been completely overtaken by fog, making him lose sight of them. Sigmund returned to Borghild's court, where he had been living, and divorced her. He then went south to his kingdom in the Franks.

Sigurd Fafnirsbane

Sigurd was the son of Hjordis, and it was apparent when he was fully grown that he had incredible physical prowess. He quickly became nurtured in the court of King Hjalprek, where he had a foster father named Regin. Regin was well-versed in exercise, magic runes, and speaking in different languages. He would teach all of these skills to Sigurd.

Gold was the driving factor in Regin's life, as he had lost out on an immense amount of gold that was part of wergild for his brother, who had been killed. The story went that Regin had two brothers, Reidmar and Fafnir. Reidmar had been killed due to a curse on some gold Loki was trying to obtain. The two surviving brothers attempted to get wergild from their father for Reidmar's death, but he refused.

Fafnir killed their father in the middle of the night and stole all of the gold he had, leaving Regin with nothing. From there, Regin went to King Hjalprek and stayed in his court as the Smith.

Meanwhile, Fafnir had a helmet and sword to defend himself and his gold hoard. He transformed himself into a venomous serpent and made a lair on Gnita Heath.

When Sigurd was old enough, Regin gave him the idea of killing Fafnir to take all of his gold. Doing this, according to Regin, would give him great renown and make him famous. Sigurd agreed and found a horse named Grani, who was a racing horse that was a descendent of Odin's horse, Sleipnir. Regin made a magnificent sword for his journey.

For some reason, the sword broke in two when Sigurd tried it, which also happened again with the second sword he was given. Sigurd's mother Hjordis, then provided him with the pieces of Sigmund's sword, which Regin crafted into the sword known as Gram.

Before Sigurd would go to kill Fafnir, he swore he would avenge his father Sigmund's death first. He ended up persuading King Hjalprek to give him an army of men and ships to kill the sons of Hunding, which he was provided with. After they set sail, they were caught in a storm, which caused them to go to land.

A man saw them land, whose name was Nikar. He asked that they call him Old Man of the Mountain, Fjolnir, or Feng instead. They brought him aboard. From there, they went out to sea again and found themselves in battle with Hunding's sons. Lyngvi was the only son they took captive, and they killed the others. However, Lyngvi did not survive for long. His ribs and lungs were both pulled out of his back, in an execution style they called a blood eagle.

Their next stop was Gnita Heath, where Fafnir was hiding. Regin gave Sigurd the idea to dig a straight trench across the path

Fafnir usually took. However, an older man gave Sigurd a better idea to dig many trenches, hiding within one of them for Fafnir.

Sigurd followed the advice of the old man and hid in one of the trenches. Within no time, Fafnir came out and spat his venom everywhere. Sigurd was able to stab his sword into Fafnir's side, giving him a mortal wound. Fafnir, hoping to get his revenge, asked for Sigurd's real name.

Even though he was apprehensive, he gave Fafnir his real name. This allowed Fafnir to put the same curse that had been put on others onto him. As soon as Sigurd obtained the gold, he would be cursed.

Regin told Sigurd that since Fafnir was his brother, he deserved wergild for his death. He wanted Fafnir's heart, which Sigurd would roast on a fire for him. Regin sliced his heart out and drank his blood before laying down to sleep.

As Sigurd roasted the heart, he touched it to see if it was done. He ended up burning himself, and instinctively put his finger in his mouth to cool. Fafnir's blood hit his tongue, and suddenly, Sigurd could understand what the birds were singing. They told him how he should be the one to eat Fafnir's heart and that he should kill Regin, as Regin wanted to betray him.

Sigurd followed the bird's warning and cut off Regin's head. He then went to the entrance of Fafnir's lair at the behest of the birds. He unburied the treasure and took all of it, strapping it to his horse. It was because of the heroic deeds that he received the surname of Fafnirsbane.

Chapter 5: The Creatures of Norse Mythology

Many creatures exist in the world of Norse mythology. From giants and elves to god-created wolves and snakes. Many would seek to harm the gods, but there exist some who would seek to help them too. This chapter will provide an insight into many of the different beasts and creatures that roam the world of Norse mythology.

Giants

Giants have a rather interesting place in Norse mythology. Many of the gods and goddesses had romances and children with giants, which is unlike other mythology where giants are seen as horrible beasts. Giants were, in some ways, seen as equal to the Aesir and Vanir gods.

However, they were not the enormous beasts modern-day people think of when they hear the word giant. Giants in Norse mythology were thought of as grand beings and were not necessarily incredibly tall. Some, like Hardgreip, were able to change their height at will, making them taller or smaller. However, most looked like regular beings, meaning that their name was largely a misnomer.

They do not have the same principals as the gods do, however. Often, they are seen on the other end of the spectrum from gods, having intertwined, yet opposing principals. It is because of this that many giants are also seen as enemies of the gods. Their original Norse name was jötnar (or singular jötunn), which means devourer.

The name giant did not come until 1066 CE when William the Conquerer took control of England. There, many French and English words mixed, including the word geant, which was the predecessor to the word giant. Geants were specifically the name for the creatures in Greek mythology who were similar to the jötnar.

There is an interesting difference between the innangard and utangard in the Germanic worldview. Innangard refers to being within the enclosure, meaning civilized and those that abide by the law. Meanwhile, utangard refers to those beyond the enclosure, specifically the chaotic and anarchic people.

Asgard would be considered innangard, as this is where the Aesir gods are enclosed. However, a place like Jotunheim, which is where the jötnar resided, would be considered utangard. Another name for Jotunheim is Utgard, which further proves that it is considered utangard.

Though the giants were at times considered enemies of the gods, they were not a group that could be easily destroyed. They offered a balance to the world, as the Aesir's duty of protection balances their ideal chaos. The Aesir simply tried to keep the giants balanced.

The devourers, or giants, are always seen as trying to bring the world back to chaos while the Aesir gods are always protecting civilization. Eventually, the giants succeeded in bringing the world back into chaos through Ragnarok.

Fenrir

Fenrir is one of the most infamous wolves in all of Norse mythology, but is considered part of the jötnar, as he was the epitome of chaos. He was the child of Loki and Angrboda, a giantess. Even though he was Loki's son, the Aesir gods raised him, hoping to keep him under control.

Though the Aesir gods raised him to keep him under control, he grew at an enormous rate to the point where they could no longer keep him at bay. They attempted to chain him up three times. The first two times, he was easily able to break through the chains. However, with the third, they secured him with the strongest chains that had ever been crafted, yet they were still light to hold.

Fenrir was devious of the new chains and said he wouldn't allow them to be put on unless one of the gods put their hand in his mouth. That way, if he was unable to break them, he would bite off their hand. Tyr ended up placing his hand into Fenrir's mouth, knowing that he would lose it.

The chains were unable to be broken, and Fenrir immediately chomped his hand clean off. The gods secured the chains on a boulder and held his mouth open with a sword. The drool from his mouth became known as the river, Expectation.

He would be stuck in these chains for many years, unable to break free until Ragnarok came. There, he would break free and cause immense chaos.

In other stories, there are other wolves mentioned with different names, but many believe they were all actually Fenrir. Many of those mentioned are during Ragnarok, which had wolves completing things that were more likely to have been done by Fenrir himself. For example, there is one wolf named Skoll who ate the sun during Ragnarok and another that would eat the moon, called Hati.

Fenrir was the one to kill Odin during Ragnarok, which led Odin's son Vidar to avenge him. Vidar was able to put an end to the horrible suffering Fenrir had caused throughout Ragnarok.

Skadi

Skadi is a goddess and giantess in Norse mythology. There is some speculation that her name is related to Scandinavia, but it is not clear if her name helped create the name Scandinavia or if it was the other way around.

She spent her time residing in the mountains, specifically in her father's hall of Thrymheim, and was often referred to as the snowshoe goddess. As an avid hunter, she became the goddess of hunting and winter. The biggest symbols associated with her are the bow and arrow, skis, and snowshoes.

When Odin killed Skadi's father for kidnapping Idun, Skadi demanded retribution. She stormed into Asgard, stating she would only accept revenge or compensation for his death. At first, they offered her gold, as they were terrified of what she could do. However, she had no desire for gold, as her father had left her a lot of wealth.

Odin then decided she could pick any god to be her husband, but only by looking at their shoes. This marriage would make her a goddess. Though she had hoped to pick Baldur, she ended up choosing Njord as his shoes appealed to her the most. They had a rather short marriage, as neither wanted to live where the other lived.

There are numerous theories about who she may have married after her and Njord's divorce. Some believed she might have married Ullr, as he was the god of archery and winter. Others believed she may have married Odin and had many children with him.

Ymir

Ymir was considered the first giant, and was a hermaphrodite. He was born after ice from Niflheim, and fire from Muspelheim converged in the abyss at Ginnungagap. This was said to have happened during the creation of the cosmos. Therefore, he is the ancestor to all of the giants in Norse mythology.

Audhumla was a cow that Ymir suckled upon to gain nourishment. Other giants were created asexually from his body as he slept, and came from his legs and the sweat in his armpits. Audhumla would lick a salty rock for her nourishment. After 3 days of wearing down the salt rocks, she uncovered Buri, who was the first of the Aesir gods.

From Buri, was made a son named Borr. Borr then mated with Bestla, who was one of Ymir's many descendants. They made not only Odin but also his two brothers, Vili and Ve. The three brothers then killed Ymir and used his body parts to create the cosmos.

In many ways, Ymir was the origination of the chaos that giants were known for. Ymir and the Ginnungagap are also something the Viking people would talk about when they were speaking of a time before the world had been created.

Hel

Hel was a giantess and goddess who presided over the underworld, which was also called Hel. Hel means "hidden," which is conducive to how the bodies of the dead were hidden in the underworld.

She is one of the children of Loki, whose mother was Angrboda, a giantess. This meant she was the sister of Fenrir and Jormungand, two of the most dangerous creatures in Norse mythology.

Hel is generally seen as a very greedy and harsh goddess, who has an indifference to both the living and the dead. Though she was the one to preside over the underworld, she is unfortunately not mentioned very many times in the remaining texts that have survived.

Some believe she may not have been a goddess at all, but was simply a personification of the grave. This was because there are not many mentions of her in the surviving stories. There is also little evidence that she was worshipped like other gods from this time.

She was most prominently mentioned in the tale of The Death of Baldur, as other gods had attempted to bring Baldur back from the underworld. However, Hel would not allow someone to leave the underworld easily. She said she would release Baldur if every living thing in the cosmos wept for him.

All but a single giantess cried for him, who was most likely Loki in disguise. Because this giantess did not cry for Baldur, Hel kept Baldur in the underworld.

Jormungand

Also known as the Midgard Serpent, Jormungand was an enormous serpent that could encircle the entirety of Midgard. He is the son of Loki and Angrboda, making him the sibling of Fenrir and Hel.

Out of all the gods, Thor is his number one enemy. They battled each other at least twice, with bot battles being documented in the Eddas. He is also the largest of all the monsters in Norse mythology.

His personality is rather dark, spending most of his time underneath the sea. This was due to Odin casting him down into the sea after he was born because he was terrified of him. The times he did surface, he was often angry and destructive.

Many continental Germans, until sometime in the Middle Ages, believed that earthquakes were created by Jormungand getting angry.

Surt

The fire god Surt was the leader of the giants when he and his kin attacked the Aesir and Vanir gods during Ragnarok. He has a sword that is burning with an incredible fire. He came from Muspelheim, which was the southernmost region filled with fire and heat.

During Ragnarok, he was fated to battle with Freyr. They both end up killing the other, which had been fated from the beginning of time.

A historian by the name of Rudolf Simek believes that Surt was the personification of the volcanoes in the underworld. Because of this, he would have held a special place in the hearts of the Icelandic people, since Iceland has many active volcanoes.

Nidhogg

"He Who Strikes with Malice" is one of the meanings behind the name of Nidhogg. He was the most prominent serpent or dragon who dwelled underneath the world tree Yggdrasil. These serpents spend a lot of time attacking and eating the roots of the Yggdrasil, which causes many injuries to the tree.

These injuries were meant to slowly bring the world back into chaos, which is why they are a part of the giant category.

Nidhogg plays a part in the tale of Ragnarok. There is a small mention of him in an Old Norse poem, "Insight of the Seeress," where he comes out from underneath Yggdrasil to likely aid the giants during Ragnarok.

He presides over Nastrond, which is a part of the underworld. This particular part of the underworld is specifically where perjurers, adulterers, and murderers are sent to be punished. It should be noted, however, that the Norse and Germanic peoples did believe in moral retribution in the way that this poem states. Therefore, this may have had some Christian influence.

Skoll and Hati

These are two wolves who were only mentioned in passing, but were primarily the two wolves who devoured the sun and moon during Ragnarok. Skoll means "One Who Mocks," and Hati means "One Who Hates," which is suiting considering what their roles were in Ragnarok.

There are conflicting ideas as to which one devoured the moon and which one devoured the sun. The historian Snorri Sturluson stated that it was Skoll who got the sun and Hati who got the moon. However, the Eddic poem called Grimnismál suggests that it was the other way around.

In one poem, Lokasenna, Fenrir is called Hroorsvitnir, which is the same name given to Hati's father. Therefore, some believe he may have been the father of Hati and Skoll. Since there is not more evidence, though, it is impossible to make this connection properly.

Aegir and Ran

Interestingly, these two are the most often mentioned out of all the giants. Unfortunately, even with all these mentions, there is still not a significant amount of information about them.

They are husband and wife, Aegir being the male, and Ran being the female. They are tied directly to the sea, as they live in a great hall under the sea and can see the power of the ocean. Aegir translates explicitly to "ocean," while Ran translates to "robber."

In the times where they are mentioned, Aegir is generally seen as a gracious host. Ran, on the other hand, is a little more sinister than Aegir. Specifically, she has been linked to the drownings of seafarers who she then drags down into her fortress.

These two had a very friendly relationship with the Aesir gods, unlike some of the other giants. For example, the Aesir gods were often asked to join Aegir and Ran at the supreme feasts they held in their hall. It is in stark contrast to the other giants with whom the Aesir gods regularly had battles.

They were claimed to have nine daughters together. These daughters are named Himminglaeva, Ud, Bölge, Kolga, Hefring, Dröfn, Blodughadda, Dufa, and Hrönn and are said to be the spirits of the waves.

Garm

Garm has very few mentions within the remaining texts. Garm is known as either a dog or a wolf who was associated with the forces of destruction and the underworld.

One of the poems in the Poetic Edda, Grimnismál, alludes that Garm is the greatest among all canines in Norse mythology. This is similar to how Odin is considered the greatest among the Aesir gods.

In both the Grimnismál and Völuspá, Garm is referred to as two different creatures: a dog in the first and a wolf in the second. This makes his animal identity a little difficult to confirm, and also has caused some to believe he may have been Fenrir all along.

There are instances where Garm does things that sounds more like the actions of Fenrir. For example, in Ragnarok, there is an instance where Garm is said to be breaking free, just as Fenrir had done himself. However, there is no concrete evidence that can point to both Garm and Fenrir being the same character.

Elves

In Norse mythology, Elves are seen as somewhat of a demigod creature. They were considered "luminous" beings, making them more beautiful than even the sun. Often, they ended up being linked to the Aesir and Vanir gods, which only made them higher in status. However, it was hard to distinguish the lines between elves, gods, giants, and other Norse beings as it was likely the Germanic people themselves saw little to no difference between them.

There are instances where elves are stated to be distinct from the Vanir gods, but there are also instances where they are stated as being the same. Freyr, one of the Vanir gods, lived in Alfheim, which was the homeland of the elves. In what capacity he lived there, it is not clear.

Elves and humans did not get along at all. It was thought that elves were causing illnesses in humans, but they could also heal them. They were more willing to heal them if they were offered sacrifices.

There were two distinct elven races: the light elves and the dark elves. The light elves were the ones who lived in Alfheim while the dark elves lived in Svartalfheim. Thus, the dark elves were given the name of dwarves. They preferred living underground while the light elves preferred living in the heavenly realm.

They starkly contrasted each other in many ways, from their personalities to their skin tone. The light elves had extremely light skin, which is why they were thought to have luminous skin. Meanwhile, the dark elves had black skin, likely as a result of them living underground for as long as they did.

Even though the dark elves were the opposite of the light elves, they still produced magic, just not in the same way as the light elves. They were primarily focused on creating objects, like weapons and jewelry, and imbuing them with magical properties.

Humans and elves were allowed to procreate together, creating half-human, half-elf offspring. These children would look just like a human but would have the magical abilities that elves did, making them intuitive and extremely powerful. After death, humans could have the chance to become elves, meaning there was a major overlap with worshiping the elves and worshiping their human ancestors.

After the Germanic people completely converted to Christianity, the worship of elves did not cease, even though it was forbidden. It continued for many, many years, lasting even longer than the worship of the gods.

Dwarves

As discussed in the previous section, dwarves were dark elves. They had pitch-black skin and preferred to live underground in Svartalfheim. This realm, which was one of the Nine Worlds, was thought to be a labyrinth of forges and mines, which made a lot of sense considering what they spent their time creating.

Though the contemporary view of dwarves is that they are small in stature, there was no indication the dwarves of Norse mythology were thought to be the same. By all accounts, they were tall and humanoid.

Above all, the dwarves were famous for their incredible ability to forge magnificent pieces in their forges. Mjolnir, likely one of the most famous Norse weapons, was crafted by the dwarves for Thor. They also crafted Gleipnir, which were the chains that fully bound Fenrir; Skidbladnir, which was Freyr's impressive ship that could fold up and always had the perfect wind; and Gungnir, which was Odin's spear that would never miss its mark.

It was said that the four corners of the sky were held up by dwarves. Their names were Austri (East), Vestri (West), Nordi (North), and Sudri (South).

Land Spirits

Just as the name implies, these were spirits who dwelled over certain landmarks in the world. They have a lot of influence over the place where they dwell. This includes influencing the well-being of the area. Their influence goes a step further also to include the well-being of those who depend on that land. These spirits were often depicted living in particularly beautiful rocks and boulders.

Depending on the person and what they do, they can bless or curse someone who walks on their land. In turn, that person could also bless or curse the land spirit, depending on how they felt.

These spirits were incredibly over-protective of their land to the point where someone disrespecting it or dishonoring it in any way would be cursed. Their passion for their land also bleeds into the rest of their personality, making them passionate about everything.

During the pre-Christianity period, the Germanic people were extremely mindful of this and maintained the land. They had no desire to lose favor with the land spirit. In Iceland, the first law code erected in 930 CE stated that when coming to land, a ship's crew needed to remove all dragon heads from the ship. Otherwise, the dragon head may frighten the land spirits.

Like elves, people continued to worship land spirits for a very long time after Christianity came into the picture. There are still some areas of the world today, particularly in Iceland, that make sure to maintain the land where land spirits are believed to dwell. One particular rock in Iceland called Grimsborg is one of these sacred places.

Draugr

The draugr are the ghosts of the dead. These people were not happy living in their graves and preferred to roam the world. But, they were not content with simply walking amongst the living.

They would create illnesses among the living and harass them, which could eventually lead to insanity or death. More than anything, these unsatisfied people were people who had done some type of evil deed when they were alive. This version could have been influenced by the early Christian writings on Norse mythology.

These creatures were not like regular ghosts, and instead had full control of their body. They were able to physically do the same things that a regular living human could, but with much more power.

They possessed super-human strength and, like the zombies of the contemporary world, had an undeniable smell of death and decay. If they were not among those who wished to torment the living, they might have wanted to guard their treasure specifically. They were also able to change their size at will and were much heavier than a regular living human was.

There was one particular story of an early settler whose name translated to 'twist-foot'. He had been buried on a ridge above a fjord, but he refused to stay buried. His ghost went after farmers, terrifying them and killing their sheep. This man's son reburied him on the other side of the mountain, out of view of the farms. For extra measure, he built a grand wall separating them.

Valkyries

The Valkyrie are among some of the most well-known creatures in Norse mythology. They were spirits who were entirely female that would aid Odin when he needed them, especially in Valhalla. In contemporary times, they are depicted as beautiful and noblewomen who ride on dead horses. This depiction is fairly accurate to what the Germanic people would have believed.

Their main daily purpose was bringing dead heroes to Valhalla after a great battle. These heroes would have been the heroes Odin had chosen as his half, with Freya receiving the other half. The word Valkyrie means "chooser of the fallen," which is fitting for what their primary role was.

Even though they have a very important warrior role in Norse mythology, later writings also indicated they had many affairs with human men. Not only that, but there were also writings about how they were Odin's personal shield-maidens. They were the servers of food and drink to the heroes in Valhalla, but this was not seen to be a lower-class duty.

Queens in Norse culture would serve the guests at banquets who held a high status. This was a way of showing respect for the things they had done. This was exactly the way the Valkyrie were depicted.

There was also a different name for them when they were on the battlefield, which was swan-maiden. They were always required to wear their plumage, for if they were caught without it, they would be trapped on earth.

In addition to their duties of choosing the fallen heroes for passage to Valhalla, they also had a more sinister duty in the early Norse writings. They would also be the choosers of which men would die in battle. To ensure those men would definitely die, the Valkyrie would use magic against them.

This side of the Valkyries was not exclusive to the Norse people. Other cultures had similar creatures to the Valkyries, who were instrumental in deciding who was to live and who was to die on the battlefield, including the Anglo-Saxons and the Celts.

Valkyries are by-and-large a projection of parts of Odin. This means they had their own bodies and minds but were still part of Odin.

The Kraken

It would not be a complete list of the Norse creatures without mentioning the Kraken. It is a legendary sea monster that has been depicted numerous times in the modern era. The Norse people believed it was at least a mile long and lived on the bottom of the sea. It would surface when it grew hungry, but would also surface if a large ship disturbed it.

The earliest mention of a beast like the Kraken was in the 13th century. This was technically after the time of the Vikings. This monster was called Hafgufa, which was believed to live deep in the ocean off the coast of Greenland. Though there is little to no evidence the Norse people themselves had a story of a grand sea monster, it would not be surprising if they did.

The Kraken looks like an enormous octopus or squid and has eyes that could be the size of dinner plates. Some say it could be mistaken for an island. The Kraken seemed to be a monster that only became grander with time. By the 15th and 16th centuries, sailors would depict the Kraken on their maps, making sure to warn others of dangerous waters.

Chapter 6: The Four Most Famous Tales of Norse Mythology

Many incredible tales come from the time of the Germanic peoples and the Vikings. From the creation of the entire world to different tales about the gods, the myths are numerous. Below are four of the most famous tales that come from Norse mythology and what they meant to the people of that time.

The Creation of the Cosmos

To the Norse people, before there was anything, there was Ginnungagap, which was an abyss of darkness. This abyss was full of chaos, yet it was also perfectly silent. It was in-between Muspelheim, which was the home of fire, and Niflheim, which was the home of ice.

Slowly, Muspelheim and Niflheim came together, meeting in Ginnungagap. The fire melted the ice, and the droppings of water came together to form Ymir, who was the first of the giants. Ymir was able to reproduce asexually and was considered a hermaphrodite. As he slept, giants came from his legs and the sweat coming from his armpits. Those giants would be among the giants the Norse people knew.

Audhumla was a cow who came from the melting ice of Niflheim. She allowed Ymir to suckle from her, giving him much needed nourishment. As more of the ice melted, salt licks appeared, which was exactly what Audumla needed to get her own nourishment.

After a long time, the licking of the salt licks would uncover Buri. Buri was considered the first of the Aesir gods; other giants had reproduced during this time, giving birth to Bestla. She was the daughter of the giant Bolthorn, and she married Buri. They had children of their own, Odin, Vili, and Ve.

The three children wanted to rid the world of Ymir, so they slaughtered him, cutting his body into pieces. They, in turn, used those pieces of his body to create the world. His blood became the oceans, his muscles and skin became the ground and soil, his hair became the green vegetation, his brains became the clouds overlooking the world, and his skull became the sky that encased the world. There were four dwarves, associated with the four cardinal directions, who held his skull above the world.

Sometime later, the gods decided they wanted to create man. So, they created the first-ever humans, Ask, and Embla. Their bodies came from tree trunks. The gods also built a large fence around Midgard, which was their homeland, to keep them safe from the destruction of the giants.

Yggdrasil

Yggdrasil is the tree that was believed to be at the center of the cosmos. Each of the Nine Worlds is attached to the world tree by the branches and roots. This way, each realm is connected, even if it is not a direct connection.

Everything in the universe is connected to the Yggdrasil. Therefore, everything relies on the health of the Yggdrasil tree to be strong and healthy. The trembling of the Yggdrasil was the first indication that Ragnarok was on the way, meaning the well-being of everything was on the line.

Various animals reside in and around the tree's trunk, branches, and roots. Darker and more dangerous animals, like snakes and the dragon named Nidhogg, are said to live around the roots of the tree, where the tree is closest to the underworld. There is an eagle that does not have a name that lives near the top in the branches. A squirrel named Ratatoskr actually climbs up and down the tree, bringing insults back and forth between the eagle and Nidhogg.

There are other animals, such as four stags named Durathror, Dvalinn, Sainn, and Duneyrr, who spend their days slowly eating away at the leaves on the branches. Though most of these animals may have a larger purpose, the imagery of the Yggdrasil being eaten away at points to its mortality.

The roots and the wells under the tree are a rather contradictory part of the tree. Different scholars and writers have claimed a different number of roots in different places; in one poem, *Grimnismál,* three main roots are protruding from the tree. The first is coming from Midgard, the land of humans. The second from Jotunheim, the land of the giants. The third from Hel, which is the underworld.

In the poem *Völuspá,* there is a singular well underneath the tree, the Well of Urd, or the Well of Fate. In the *Prose Edda,* there are actually three wells, one that attaches to each of the roots. Also, the Well of Urd is not underneath the tree, but sits in the sky. There is a root that is attached to it that also extends up into the sky.

According to the *Prose Edda,* the Well of Urd is where the gods convene their daily council meetings. A second well, called Hvergelmir, is not so much a well as it is a body of water. It is connected to the root that extends to Niflheim, where there is nothing but ice. Out of all the roots, this is the one that Nidhogg prefers to eat away at. The third well is connected to a root from the giant realm of Jotunheim. This is called Mimir, the well of the wise.

As for the Nine Worlds, there is no specific diagram that shows where each world sits on the tree. Some clues give a vague idea of where some of the realms do sit, however.

It appears that the worlds were arranged in two straight lines: one going vertically up the tree and the other representing the journey between innangard and utangard, which was horizontal. On the vertical line, Asgard would have been among the highest branches at the top of the tree. Midgard, then, would be at the base of the trunk near the roots. Finally, Hel would have been underneath the tree entangled in the roots.

For the horizontal line, it would have been the other six worlds, which included Jotunheim. Most of the other worlds were never spoken of, making it difficult to say exactly what they were. However, they would have been in line with Midgard, stretching away from the tree on either side.

As the center of all things, the Yggdrasil was incredibly important to the creation of the cosmos. It holds the balance between all of the worlds and keeps the worlds alive. Without the Yggdrasil, Ragnarok likely would have taken place much sooner than it did.

Meaning to the Norse People

Every religion has a creation story. Some of them are more violent than others, but they all are a way to convey a message to the people who follow. The creation of the cosmos is no exception.

Ymir and Ginnungagap, the abyss before Ymir was created, both symbolize chaos. They also symbolize limitless potential, things that have not yet been created or may never be created. Within Ginnungagap, life was created in the form of Ymir, Audhumla, other giants, and the first of the gods. Ymir himself was used to create the first elements of the world.

Being the first of the giants, Ymir was also what every other giant would end up portraying. He was the epitome of chaos, and all the giants that followed him shared that trait. They are the ones who are always trying to pull the world back into chaos.

When taking a look at the Viking people, there was one thing they were known for above all else: their eagerness to engage in battle. Looking at their eagerness for battle and the creation story, it comes as no surprise that the story is rooted in chaos and conflict.

Ymir, which began the whole universe as they knew it, was created when two opposing forces came into contact. Fire and ice were likely two things the Germanic people knew very well, especially in the cold lands of the North Atlantic.

Unlike in some other religions, the initial act of violence here was not seen as a bad thing. In Christianity, Cain killing Abel was a lesson on sin. However, with Odin, Vili, and Ve killing Ymir, it was considered a sacred task. This is what created the world and began the life the Germanic people were living.

While this story may make it seem like it was okay for the Vikings to kill without mercy, it was not what the story truly meant. It was a way for them to accept that taking the violent approach to life that they did take was okay. They still had laws and would not kill if it was not necessary, but they could also continue to sail and engage in acts of violence if it meant furthering their people. It was also beneficial to the heroes to obtain renown among their people.

It is also interesting to learn that both gods and giants held a place in the hierarchy. It was necessary to keep the balance of the world, and these two forces are equally matched.

To the Norse, they were living in the middle of these two forces. Midgard, where the humans lived, was often a battleground. On one side, they had goodness, law and order, and godliness. On the other side, they had chaos, evil, and profaneness. It could be looked at as though these two sides could influence certain humans one way or the other.

The Death of Baldur

As one of the most beloved gods in Norse mythology, Baldur's death was one of the hardest to deal with. There was a lot of fallout from his death, especially on the one who caused it in the first place. Though there are a few different versions of this tale, this one is among the most popular.

Baldur was the son of Odin and Frigg, one of two sons they had together. He was a generous god, always looking to help others and protect them. His courage was stronger than any other, and he was always filled with a lot of joy. Therefore, when he started having dreams about his death, he began to panic that he might die.

Odin was asked by the other gods, who were all afraid something might happen to their favorite god, to figure out what was causing his dreams. They also wanted to find out if there was any truth behind those dreams, or if the dreams should simply be ignored.

Without wasting time, Odin mounted his horse, Sleipnir, and took off for the underworld. He was hoping to speak with a seeress who had died some time ago. This seeress had been known to be wise with this sort of thing in the past.

As he was one of the Aesir gods, he could not afford to be seen in the underworld. He took on many different disguises along the way until he reached the place where the seeress was. Odin noticed the halls in the underworld had been decorated and were looking magnificent as if a party was going to take place. This was not something he would expect to see in the underworld.

Once he found the seeress, still under disguise, he awoke her and immediately asked what was going on with the decoration. She told him there was a guest of honor who would be joining them soon, which was none other than Baldur. She then proceeded to tell him how he was going to be killed and started to answer some of his questions before she realized who he truly was. After that, she refused to speak anymore, not telling him exactly how Baldur was fated to die.

Odin returned to Asgard, feeling completely defeated. He told the council, including Frigg, what he had learned in the underworld. However, Frigg was not about to just give up, no matter how likely it was that it would happen. She took off and spoke with everything in all the cosmos, asking for an oath that they would not hurt Baldur. Every entity she went to told her they would not harm him.

When she returned and spoke of what she had done, the other gods were joyous. So, they decided to make a little game out of it. They began to throw things at him, from rocks and sticks to knives and swords. Everything they threw merely bounced off of him, leaving him completely unharmed.

This game attracted the company of Loki, who was always looking to stir up trouble somewhere.

He disguised himself and decided the first thing to do was ask Frigg if she really got everything to agree to her oath. She said everything had, but she had not bothered to ask mistletoe as it was such a small and innocent thing. She did not believe it would be necessary to bother it because there was no way it could harm Baldur.

Quickly, Loki created a plan. He left Frigg and went to make a spear from the 'innocent' mistletoe tree. He brought the spear back to where the gods were and located Hodr, a god who was blind. Sneakily, Loki told Hodr that he must be feeling pretty left out, not being able to throw things at Baldur like everyone else was. Hodr, not knowing who he was talking with, confirmed that yes, he was feeling left out.

Loki handed him the spear and told him he would guide his hand to make the perfect hit. Hodr, guided by Loki's mischievous hand, threw the spear at Baldur. As soon as it hit, Baldur fell to the ground, dying from the mistletoe.

Everyone fell completely silent. Not only did their most beloved god die, but it also signified the first event in the coming of Ragnarok.

Frigg was able to compose herself enough to ask if there was anyone who would be brave enough to journey to Hel. They would need to make a deal with Hel, who was the goddess of death, to bring Baldur back to Asgard. One of Odin's lesser-known sons, Hermod, agreed to take the journey. Odin instructed his steed to bring Hermod down to the underworld.

While Hermod was journeying to the underworld, the rest of the gods prepared a grand funeral for Baldur. Some of the gods worked on turning Baldur's ship, the famous Hringhorni, into a funeral pyre. They made it even more lavish than the ship already was, making it fit for the best of kings.

However, when it was finally time to push the ship out to sea, it became stuck in the sand. They tried everything to get it out, but none of them were strong enough to push it. They called for a giantess named Hyrrokkin, who was considered the strongest in all of the cosmos, to help them push the pyre.

She arrived on a wolf with poisonous snakes for reigns. With a single push that caused the land to quake, the ship was finally in the water. As the other gods carried Baldur onto the ship, his widow Nanna became overwhelmed with emotion. She died on the spot from grief. The gods decided to put her on the ship as well, keeping them together.

Thor, using his hammer, kindled the fire that would soon overwhelm the ship. Odin placed one of his rings, Draupnir, onto the ship along with Baldur's horse. The ship slowly sailed out to sea until it was lost entirely from their sight.

An incredible amount of different beings attended the funeral, including dwarves, Valkyries, giants, and elves. Everyone had some type of connection with Baldur, as he was one of the greatest gods that ever lived. They all gathered there to mourn the loss of someone so special.

It took Hermod nine nights to reach the part of the underworld where Hel resided. He had to travel through some of the darkest and deepest valleys to get there. At one point, he reached a river called Gjoll, where a giantess named Modgud was standing guard at the bridge over Gjoll.

When she saw Hermod approach, she questioned who he was and why he was there. It was incredibly strange to have someone who was still alive with such loud and thunderous footfalls. He gave her enough of an answer to satisfy her and continued on his way, finally reaching Hel's land. Sleipnir, Odin's horse, quickly leaped over the wall that surrounded her land.

Once he was inside and spotted Hel on her throne, he dismounted Sleipnir. He could see Baldur sitting in a seat of honor right next to her, his face pale and incredibly downcast. Even though he wished to ask Hel immediately, he decided it was best to wait until the morning, and he slept by Sleipnir for the night.

In the morning, he went to Hel and begged her to allow Baldur to return to Asgard. He told her about the immense sorrow that was hanging over the heads of every living creature because of his death. It was even more pronounced among the gods, as they had grown with him and had known him since he was born.

Hel told him if everyone was truly as sad as he said they were, then he just needed to get every living thing in the cosmos to weep for Baldur. If that happened, she would return Baldur to the land of the living. However, if even one thing did not cry, then she was going to keep Baldur there forever, no matter how many others did weep for him.

Thankful for the possibility of getting him back, Hermod rushed back to Asgard to tell them exactly what she had told him. They just needed to get everything to cry for him, and he would be returned to them.

At once, they sent messengers to everything in the cosmos, telling them of this news. Everyone they spoke to did indeed end up weeping for Baldur, as he truly was loved just as much as Hermod said he was. That is, everyone except for a single giantess.

Tokk, who was ultimately Loki in disguise, refused to cry for him. She said he should stay down in the underworld and let Hel hold what she already has. Due to her refusal, Hel kept her end of the bargain. She would continue to keep Baldur in her clutches and refuse to let him leave. He would never again walk among the living, keeping the joy and light he once held at bay from the rest of the cosmos.

Vali, who was another one of Odin's children, decided they needed to avenge Baldur's death. However, they did not go after Loki, even though he was the mastermind behind it all. Instead, they went after Hodr, the blind god who had been the one to throw the spear of mistletoe in the first place. Vali killed Hodr, who was his half-brother.

Then, they went after Loki. After Loki had disguised himself as Tokk, he fled and disguised himself as a salmon, trying to stay hidden for as long as possible. He ended up going to a waterfall and staying there, believing it would be the best place to remain hidden.

However, the Aesir gods knew exactly where he was. They went to the waterfall and first attempted to catch him in a net. Loki jumped right over the net, knowing that being caught would mean the end of him. Thor anticipated Loki's action and leapt into the air, catching Loki as he was jumping over the net.

Instead of killing Loki like they had killed Hodr, they brought him to a cave and tied him up. For extra measure, they placed a snake above him, who would continuously drip venom onto his face, which caused him immense pain. Every time a drip of venom would hit him, earthquakes and other natural disasters would befall Midgard. He would remain there until Ragnarok.

Ragnarok

As with other religions, there is always a great end to the world. For the Germanic peoples, the world was bound to end in Ragnarok, the cataclysmic destruction of literally everything in the universe. To the Vikings, this tale was a prophecy of what would eventually happen, though no one was sure when it would happen.

At a time when the Norns, who were the weavers of fate, decided it should happen, the end of the cosmos would occur. First, a Great Winter would come, unlike anything anyone had ever seen before or would ever see again. Winds colder than ever would blow the snow in every single direction. The sun would not be able to penetrate the thick snow.

This winter would last as long as three regular winters, giving no summer in between. Everything would be much colder due to the lack of sun. People would become desperate for food and water, among other things, and forget the laws they had established for themselves. Everyone would focus entirely on survival, attacking their kin without remorse. Morality would be gone.

Skoll and Hati, the two wolves who were always chasing after the sun and moon to kill them, would finally catch up and be able to kill them. Stars, which were once a source of guidance in the night, would completely fade away. All that would be left in the sky would be immense darkness.

Yggdrasil, the ever-strong tree, would finally tremble. Mountains and trees would come crashing to the ground at the tremble, leaving nothing but a flat surface on which to battle. Fenrir, Loki's monstrous wolf-child, would finally break free of the chains that had been holding him back for a long time. Another one of Loki's children, Jormungand, would rise from his home at the bottom of the ocean and splash the oceans over the land as he himself hit the land. The land would eventually become completely flooded by the rising water.

All of the commotion would push Naglfar, a ship made from fingernails and toenails of the dead, out of the moorings which trapped it. As the world would be flooded, it would easily sail anywhere they needed it to go. The ship would be crewed by an army of giants and commanded by Loki, who was finally getting the chaos he yearned for. He had been able to break free from the cave they had left him in.

Fenrir would take his freedom to the ground. A fire would shoot out of his eyes and nostrils, and he would open his mouth so wide that the top hit the top of the sky, and the bottom hit the ground beneath him. He would eat everything in his path. Jormungand would spit his venom at everything he could see, whether it was water or land. This venom would poison everything it touched, even the air they breathed.

At the dome of the sky, a crack will appear. From that crack, fire-giants from Muspelheim would crawl through, lead by Surt. His flaming sword would be brighter than the sun ever was. These giants will go to and walk on the rainbow bridge named Bifrost, to Asgard, and it will shatter behind them, leaving no bridge in their wake.

Heimdall, the divine sentry of Asgard, will blow his horn Gjallarhorn to announce to everything that the moment they have been fearing was finally there. Upon hearing the horn, Odin would immediately head to the head of Mimir, who was known to be the wisest being and ask for advice on what to do next.

Even though the gods all know what will happen to them if they fight, they head into battle anyway. They go to the battlefield that is known as Vigrid, or "Plain Where Battle Surges," to fight their enemies.

As it had been foretold, Odin would go there and meet Fenrir. He would have the einherjar beside him, which were the many human warriors he chose and had kept in Valhalla for this exact moment. Odin led the warriors into battle, fighting valiantly. However, it was not his fate to survive the attack. Fenrir swallowed all of his warriors and even swallowed Odin himself.

In a rage, one of Odin's sons Vidar saw what Fenrir had done and ran to avenge his father's death. He was wearing a shoe that had been crafted using the scraps of leather that human leathermakers had thrown away. This shoe was made exactly for this moment.

Vidar kicked Fenrir's mouth open with the foot that was wearing the shoe. The shoe was powerful enough to hold open his mouth, giving Vidar the time he needed to stab Fenrir directly through the throat. Finally, after many years, Fenrir was dead.

There was another wolf by the name of Garm, who was fated to fight the god Tyr. They will end up killing each other; the same will happen to Heimdall and Loki. They will fight valiantly and die at the hand of the other. Loki's treacherous life will finally be ended.

Freyr, one of the Vanir gods who was an honorary Aesir god, will attack the giant Surt. They will also end up killing each other. Thor is fated to fight his biggest enemy, Jormungand, the giant serpent that can encircle the entire world. During this intense battle, Thor will land many blows to Jormungand. These blows will eventually be too much for Jurmungand, and he will fall to the ground dead. However, Jormungand will spend most of the fight spitting venom onto Thor. Once Jormungand is dead, Thor will walk nine paces before he, too, will die.

Eventually, the world will completely sink into the sea. Nothing will be left except for the void that had always been there. Everything that had been created since Muspelheim and Niflheim collided will be gone forever.

In some versions, this is the end. Nothing more will come after this. However, in some versions, a brand new world will emerge from the end of everything. Those who survived Ragnarok, like Thor's sons Modi and Magni, and Odin's son Vali, will live without any problems in the new world.

There will be a man and woman, named Lif and Lifthrasir, who hid themselves during Ragnarok; they are the last living humans left on earth and will come out of hiding when the new world is born. They hid in the "Wood of Hoddmimir" but will leave to populate the new world.

Not only will there be new life on earth, but also a new life in the sky. The daughter of the previous sun will come into the sky and take the place of her father, breathing warmth and life into the new world. And, though they are not given a name, everything will be watched over by a new supreme ruler who takes Odin's spot.

Meaning to the Norse People

There are essentially two versions of the end of Ragnarok. In one version, nothing else happens after the end of the world, and in another there is a brand new world that is born. It is possible that the version without rebirth was the original Norse ending. They did not believe there would be anything else. Then, what does that mean for the version with a rebirth?

Some believe the rebirth may have been written as part of the Christian influence. At the end of the Christian bible, the world is destroyed and it gives birth to paradise. Therefore, it would be entirely plausible that Christianity influenced this rebirth in Norse mythology. Another possibility is that they wanted to show the changes the Norse people were going through. They were completely changing their religion to Christianity, so their old religion had to die, just like the world had to end in Ragnarok.

Regardless of what interpretation may be true, the story of Ragnarok was incredibly important to the Viking people.

Reading through this tale, it seems like it is a rather tragic ending. Many of the gods they knew and loved were destined to die. Many times, they died at the hand of their greatest enemy. They also knew in their hearts that one day, which could have been during their lifetime, this was the end the world would eventually face.

Though it may seem hopeless to modern audiences, for the Vikings, it was inspirational. This story showed how the gods were just as mortal as they were. They would one day cease to exist, just as humans were fated to. However, the gods did not go out with their hearts heavy and heads low. They went out fighting until their last breath.

The Vikings wanted to follow this mentality. They could not be afraid of their inevitable death. Instead, they would go into every fight knowing it may be their last but fighting anyway. They would continue to do noble deeds and not freeze at the idea of their death.

Chapter 7: Other Tales from Norse Mythology

Many fascinating tales come from Norse mythology. Beyond the creation and destruction of the world, there are a bunch of other tales that were not only thought-provoking for the Germanic peoples, but also helped them understand the gods just a little bit more.

A lot of stories have been lost over the years, but there are still a bunch of key tales that we know helped the Germanic people in their day to day lives. Some of those stories are detailed in this chapter.

Discovery of the Runes

Odin was always looking to gain more knowledge. He always yearned for more and more experience and would do anything to obtain that knowledge, even once giving his eye up for more insight.

The runes were the letters that the Norse and Germanic peoples used as their alphabet. This was before the introduction of the Latin alphabet in the Middle Ages. The runes were much more significant than only being the letters they used to write. They were said to be the symbols of the most powerful forces in the universe. The term rune actually has a double meaning in Germanic languages, meaning both 'letter' and 'secret'.

They believed these runes were not only an alphabet and a way to communicate but also a way to interact with the power from the forces the runes represented. Odin believed this to be an incredibly important thing to give to the people of Midgard.

Yggdrasil grows from the Well of Urd, or the Well of Life. This well is impossibly deep and is the home to an immense number of magical forces and beings. Three of those beings are known as the Norns. They are maidens who are tasked with crafting the fate of every living thing in the cosmos. The technique they use most frequently is the art of carving runes into the trunk of Yggdrasil. These runes are designed to push the fate of all things through Yggdrasil and into each of the Nine Worlds.

Odin spent much of his time watching the Norns while they worked. He would sit in Asgard on his throne and slowly grow envious of the power that the Norns possessed. He decided he needed to know everything that they knew and gain their powers.

He was well-aware that the runes would not present themselves to anyone except to those who proved themselves. So, he decided to hang himself from one of the branches of Yggdrasil and stab his body with his spear to prove his worth. He stared down into the depths of the Well of Urd, waiting for the runes to come to him.

He did not allow any of the gods to get him food or water. He also forbade them from helping him in any way. He knew the only way to get what he wanted was on his own.

For nine days and nights, he hung from the Yggdrasil, staring down into the water of the well. He was on edge, not quite alive, but also not yet dead. At the end of the ninth night, there was movement in the water. Finally, the runes showed themselves to Odin. They had decided his sacrifice was more than worth showing him their forms and the secrets that they held.

Odin immediately worked on memorizing everything they were showing him. Once he was confident he would not forget, he cut himself from the tree and took the spear from his body.

Once he held the knowledge of the runes, he became the most formidable being in the universe. The magic from the runes flowed into him, giving him the ability to heal wounds, both mind and body, allowing him to defeat his enemies by making their weapons worthless, and even more incredible things.

The Mead of Poetry

After the end of the Aesir-Vanir War, gods and goddesses from both sides came together in order to seal the peace pact they made. They each spit into a vat to seal the truce. All of the spit came together to form a new being named Kvasir. He was considered the wisest human that ever lived. Any question people brought to him, he would be able to give a good answer in return.

At some point, after he became very famous, he was invited to the home of Fjalar and Galar, who were dwarves. Right when he got there, the dwarves killed Kvasir. They took his blood and brewed it into a mead. The mead held his ability to give wisdom to the person who drank it, and it was aptly named Óðrœrir, or Stirrer of Inspiration.

The gods immediately went to the dwarves and demanded to know what happened to Kvasir, as he had completely disappeared. The dwarves simply said that he choked on his wisdom, keeping their secret safe.

However, this was only the beginning of the killing for these dwarves. They loved the feeling they got when they killed Kvasir and decided to continue killing others. A giant named Gilling was their next victim. They took him on a ship out to sea and drowned him, simply because they wanted to.

Gilling's wife was mourning so loudly that the dwarves grew annoyed, so they killed her as well. They dropped a large millstone on top of her head when she walked under a doorway in their house.

Gilling had a son named Suttung. When he found out what had happened to his father, he captured the dwarves and carried them out to a reef during low tide. That same reef would be overwhelmed by water when high tide came. The dwarves begged for their lives. When they said they would give him the mead of Kvasir's blood, he decided to let them go.

He hid the mead underneath a mountain called Hnitbjorg and told his daughter Gunnlod she needed to be the one to guard it.

Odin, of course, heard about the mead that could grant the drinker the knowledge of a poet or scholar. In his pursuit of more knowledge, he grew upset that the mead had been hidden away from everyone and everything. It was then that he decided he would have the mead and give it only to himself, and to others who he determined to be worthy.

He then proceeded to disguise himself as a farmhand and go to the farm that Sutting's brother, Baugi, owned. On the farm, nine servants were mowing the hay in the fields. Odin went up to them and took a whetstone out of his cloak. He offered to sharpen all of their scythes to make their job a little easier.

The sharpening was like magic. The scythes were able to cut much better than they had before, and the servants all asked if they could buy the whetstone, as they all believed it to be the greatest whetstone in the world. Odin said he would be willing to sell it, but it would be for a very high price.

He threw the whetstone into the air in the middle of all the servants. He then watched as they all rushed towards the stone. In their rush to catch the stone, they ended up killing each other with their scythes.

After watching them kill each other, he then went to Baugi's door and knocked. When he answered, Odin, claimed to be someone named Bölverkr, which translates to "Worker of Misfortune." He said that he was willing to do the work of the nine servants that Baugi had. He also told him that he watched the servants kill each other in the field over a dispute. Instead of being paid, he demanded a sip from the mead he knew Sutting had.

Though Baugi was Sutting's brother, he had no control over the mead, which is exactly what he told Odin. He also told him how Sutting was very protective of it and wanted no one to see it. That being said, he said if it was true that he could do the work of nine men, then he would help him get the mead he desired.

As he was a god, doing the work of nine men was easy enough. By the end of the growing season, he had completely fulfilled his promise and accompanied Baugi to meet his brother. When they arrived and asked about getting a sip of the mead, Sutting grew incredibly angry and completely refused.

When they left, Odin reminded Baugi of their deal and convinced him to help him enter Gunnlod's dwelling where the mead was hidden. They went to the part of the mountain they knew to be closest to the chamber underneath.

Odin pulled an auger from his cloak and gave it to Baugi to drill through the mountain. Baugi got to work immediately and eventually said that he had gotten to the other side. Odin, however, did not believe him. He went up to the hole and blew into it. The rock dust blew back into his face, meaning the hole was still not all the way through.

Annoyed, he demanded that Baugi finish what he had started. Baugi completed the work with the auger and once again said the hole was complete. So, Odin blew into the hole for a second time, but this time the dust did not blow back into his face. The hole was truly complete.

He thanked Baugi for his help and then transformed himself into a snake and slithered through the hole quickly. Baugi attempted to stab after him with the auger, but Odin was already far enough away.

On the other side, Odin transformed again, this time to a charming young man. He walked towards where Gunnlod was known to be guarding the mead and began to charm her. It did not take long before he was able to win her over. She promised him that if he slept with her for three nights, she would allow him to take three sips of mead.

Desiring the mead, he agreed and slept with her for three nights. After the third night, he went to where the mead was hiding. The mead was sitting in three vats. He took a sip from each, which was a large enough sip to drink all of it completely.

One last time, he transformed himself into an eagle and immediately took off for Asgard. However, it did not take long for Sutting to realize what had happened. He transformed himself into an eagle as well and followed Odin all the way back to Asgard.

The other gods in Asgard saw Odin approaching, but they also saw Sutting not too far behind him. Many of them went out to the rim of their stronghold in preparation for an attack. However, Odin was faster than Sutting and managed to pass the border before him. Knowing there was no way he could take on all of Asgard, he retreated.

Odin made his way to a container and regurgitated the mead he had swallowed. A few droplets missed the container and fell down to Midgard. The people who these droplets hit would become some of the worst poets and scholars in the world. The truly amazing poets and scholars would be the ones who received the mead from Odin personally.

The Aesir-Vanir War

Freya was always known to practice seidr, a very powerful kind of magic that could be corruptive. Just like others who had mastered seidr, she often went into towns and villages, being paid to use her magic for the benefit of others.

After many years, she took the name Heiðr and traveled to Asgard, which was the home of the Aesir gods. When she performed her magic, the Aesir gods were completely enraptured. They immediately started giving her requests for her magic. It did not take them long to realize they were disregarding their values, including their honor, loyalty, and obedience to their kin. They were too busy looking to fulfill the many selfish requests they had with Freyr's magic.

Once they became awakened to their shortcomings, they began to call her Gullveig, which means Gold-greed, and they attempted to murder her. They decided to burn her for the witch that she was. However, the three times they tried to burn her, she came back to life each time, being reborn from the ashes.

Due to this attempted murder of Freya, the Aesir and Vanir gods began to despise each other. The hatred they felt only grew as time went on, all the way to the point where they went to war. The Vanir gods decided to attack the Aesir gods using the magic they were known for. The Aesir gods, however, were much more interested in regular combat, using weapons and hand-to-hand combat.

This war continued for a long time, with each side gaining the upper hand at different points. After many years, both sides began to grow incredibly weary of all the fighting they had been doing. They then decided to call a truce between both of their tribes.

The customary tradition of trading hostages as tribute after a truce was common among the ancient Germanic peoples. This tradition was upheld with the two tribes. Freya, Freyr, and Njord from the Vanir tribe went over to the Aesir tribe. From the Aesir tribe, Hoenir and Mimir were sent over to the Vanir tribe.

Njord and his two children, Freya and Freyr, lived peacefully in the Aesir tribe. Hoenir and Mimir, however, were not treated nearly as well in the Vanir tribe. Hoenir was someone who could provide incredibly wise advice for anyone who asked, but was unable to do this when he was not with Mimir. The people of the Vanir tribe did not realize he needed Mimir to access the wise advice.

Hoenir was very simple-minded without Mimir and would often be at a loss for words. Any time the Vanir would ask him for advice on what to do, he would not know how to respond and would likely only say, "Let others decide." They grew to believe they had been completely cheated in the exchange of hostages.

In their anger, they cut Mimir's head off and sent just the head back to Asgard and the Aesir gods. Odin was heartbroken over the loss of Mimir. He used some quick thinking with magic and embalmed it within some herbs. This preserved Mimir enough so that he would still be able to give Odin knowledge during difficult times.

Even though they normally would have gone to war over what had happened with Mimir, they were still tired from the previous war. Instead, they decided to all spit into a cauldron one by one. The saliva formed together to create Kvasir, who was the wisest of all beings in the universe.

The Fortification of Asgard

For many years, there was no wall around Asgard. One day, a smith, who was a giant, came to Asgard, and he asked the gods if they would like him to build a wall around their city. With this high wall, it would be able to keep out those who want to attack them. He stated he would be able to complete all of the work within three seasons. However, it would not be cheap.

He would take nothing less than marrying the goddess Freya, and both the sun and moon as payment.

The gods came together and discussed the smith's proposal. Freya was completely against the entire thing, especially the compensation he demanded. Loki, however, had an idea. He said they would consent to his demands, but only if he were to complete his work in one winter rather than three seasons and only if he were to do it without any help except his horse.

They talked it over, trying to figure out if that may have been the best idea. In the end, they decided it was their only option. None of the gods had any desire to give up Freya, the sun, or the moon, so they believed the impossible was the best way to make sure it did not happen.

Much to their surprise, the smith actually agreed to their proposal. However, he needed them to swear an oath that as long he did finish in the proposed time period, they would keep their end of the bargain. This oath would also ensure that he would remain safe in Asgard during the duration of his work.

Soon after, he began his work on the wall. He moved incredibly fast, much more quickly than they had been expecting. Even more impressive was his horse, who was named Svadilfari, or Unlucky Traveler. He was able to build the wall even faster than the smith was working. The stallion would often haul incredibly heavy boulders across incredibly long distances to the wall.

With three days left to the end of the winter, the wall was nearly complete. All that was left were the stones that needed to be laid around the gate. The wall itself was incredibly strong and basically impenetrable against nearly any enemy Asgard may end up facing.

The gods were completely baffled at how quickly everything had happened. They immediately turned on Loki and demanded to know why he had given them such terrible advice. They threatened him with death if he was unable to find a way to stop the giant from finishing his work. They refused to lose Freya, the sun, and the moon, especially since it would condemn the world to darkness.

Loki, in his normal self-preservation mode, pleaded with the gods to allow him to live. He promised he would figure out a way to stop the smith from finishing his work.

Later that night, both the smith and his horse went out into a snowy forest in search of the stones they needed. During their journey, they came into contact with a mare, who was Loki in disguise. The mare whinnied at the stallion from afar. The stallion was completely overcome with desire for the mare.

He broke his reins and immediately went after the mare. Loki, disguised as the mare, ran through the woods the entire night, the stallion chasing after him with hot desire. When morning finally came, the stallion was still missing. The giant knew he would never be able to finish the wall on time without his horse.

When the smith returned to Asgard and the time ran out, the gods paid him the compensation they believed he deserved. Thor smashed his hammer against his head hard enough to shatter it into pieces that were the size of breadcrumbs.

In the forest, Svadilfari was finally able to catch up with the mare that he had lusted after. They mated, and Loki gave birth to a gray horse with eight legs named Sleipnir. This horse would eventually become Odin's horse.

Odin's Quest for Wisdom

One of Odin's first quests to gain wisdom was to the Well of Urd. He was obsessed with learning, and was willing to do practically anything to gain more knowledge.

He went to the roots of the Yggdrasil and ventured down to the Well of Urd. There, he was able to find the being named Mimir, who was a shadow figure. Mimir was the guardian of the well and all the knowledge it could provide. He was incredibly knowledgeable, having knowledge that was nearly unparalleled in the universe. This knowledge came from drinking the water of the well over many years.

Right after Odin arrived, he asked Mimir if he could have a drink from the well. However, Mimir knew exactly what power the well could provide, and refused to give him any of the water. He stated that Odin would need to give one of his eyes in return.

It is not clear if Odin made his decision quickly or anguished over it for a time, but in the end, he decided it was worth it. He gouged his eye out and dropped it into the well. Mimir was satisfied with the sacrifice. He grabbed his horn and dipped it into the water, allowing Odin to drink from the well.

There is no surviving detail of what knowledge Odin gained from the well, but many scholars have guessed at what it may have been. Some believe he may have received some type of enhanced perception. Whether it was in his other eye or some other kind of perception, there is no way of knowing for sure.

The Binding of Loki

After the death of Baldur and before they were able to catch him, Loki slandered the gods at every opportunity. This went on for many years before the gods finally decided they had enough of his attitude. It was then that they decided to capture him and hold him hostage to keep him from doing anything bad ever again.

When he heard of their decision, he ran as far from Asgard as he could. He went to the peak of an incredibly high mountain and built himself a house that had four doors. This way, he would be able to look outside and see anyone who may be looking for him from any direction.

During the days, he would transform himself into a salmon and hide in a waterfall that was near his house. At night, he would sit around a fire and weave a net that he would catch fish with.

Odin, of course, was able to see where Loki was hiding from incredibly far away. He told the gods of the location, and they immediately went looking for him. Loki was able to see them coming from far away thanks to the four doors he had created in his house. When he saw them, he threw the net he had been working on into the fire and immediately transformed into a salmon, jumping into the waterfall he frequented.

However, the gods were not tricked that easily. When they saw the net burning in the fire, they assumed he was likely hiding as a fish. They then took the twine that Loki had been using to make his nets and crafted up their own net.

They went to the closest stream, where they assumed Loki would be hiding, and began to toss their net into the water. They tossed it in numerous times, but the salmon that Loki was transformed into always dodged it.

However, Loki grew impatient. He desired his freedom too much and decided to leap over the net in order to swim downstream to the sea. What he was not expecting was for Thor to catch him with his bare hands. He tried to get out of his hands, but Thor held on strongly to the tailfins of the salmon.

Having been transformed back to his regular form, he was escorted to a cave. They also went and got his two sons, transforming one into a wolf and having him slaughter the other one, leaving his insides throughout the cave.

They transformed the entrails of his dead son into heavy iron chains, using them to bind him to three large rocks. One of the gods, Skadi, put a poisonous snake on top of a rock by his head. This way, the venom from the snake would slowly drip onto Loki's head.

Sigyn, who was Loki's wife, immediately came to his side. She was always incredibly loyal to him and did not want to see him endure any pain. So, she held a bowl above his head right in front of the snake's mouth to catch the venom as it fell. After a while, the bowl would fill, and she would need to leave the cave to dispose of the contents. During those times, the venom would drip onto Loki's head, causing immense pain and discomfort.

The pain he felt would translate to Midgard, where earthquakes would shake the entirety of the world. Until Ragnarok, this is where Loki and Sigyn would remain.

The Binding of Fenrir

Loki had three children with the giantess Angrboda, all of whom were monstrous in their own ways. First was Jormungand, who was a giant serpent that could wrap around Midgard. Next was Hel, who was the death-goddess in the underworld, and third was Fenrir, a giant and fearsome wolf.

After each of these children were born, the other gods would get feelings of foreboding. They were not sure exactly what it was, but they knew they could not trust them. They were correct in their thinking, as all three would have a hand in Ragnarok, both before and during. Jormungand would kill Thor, Hel would refuse to send Baldur back to the land of the living, and Fenrir would eat Odin on the battlefield.

Trusting their gut instinct, they decided to separate them and put them as far away from each other as possible. Jormungand was tossed down to Midgard, throwing him into the sea. Hel was sent to the underworld, where she would end up thriving. As for Fenrir, they were too afraid to let him out of their sight. They decided to attempt to raise him themselves, hoping he may be better than they feared when he was fully grown.

One of the gods, Tyr, was always a strong believer in the law. He wanted it to be upheld at all times. He was also the only one out of all the gods who would dare get close enough to Fenrir to feed him.

Fenrir grew at an exceptionally fast rate, much faster than they believed he would. The gods decided that he could no longer stay in Asgard with how large he was growing. They were also well-aware that they could not allow him to roam freely, so their only choice was to bind him.

The only reason they were able to get his consent to try to put the chains on him was by telling him that it was a test of his strength. They tried several different chains, yet they would continue to break every time they put them on him.

After many unsuccessful attempts with the chains, the gods eventually sent a messenger to Svartalfheim, which was the realm of the dwarves. They were among the most skilled at crafting different items, both weapons, and tools.

The dwarves went and forged chains that were stronger than any chain that had been built before. They stated these would be the world's strongest chains and that they would be able to withstand the ferocity of Fenrir. They crafted them out of the beard of a woman, a fish's breath, a mountain's roots, the sound of a cat's footsteps, and a bird's spittle. They were all things that technically did not exist, which is why it was futile to struggle against it.

The chain's name was Gleipnir, and it was deceivingly light, yet felt strong. They presented these new chains to Fenrir, who immediately became suspicious. He outright refused to be bound with the new chains unless they consented to his demand. He would only allow them to bind him if one of the gods would put their hand into his mouth. This way, if the chains did hold his strength, he would be able to bite their hand off in retribution.

All of the gods were against the idea completely. They knew they would lose their hand if they did what he asked. That was, until Tyr, who was always braver than the others, said he would do it. He put his hand into Fenrir's mouth as the other gods bound him with the chains.

Just as the dwarves had promised, the chains were strong enough to hold him. Fenrir was bound entirely. He immediately chomped Tyr's hand off and swallowed it whole.

Now that he was bound, they sent him to an incredibly lonely place that was far from anything. They bound him to a boulder and put a sword inside his jaws to keep them wide open. The despair that he felt caused him to howl extremely loudly and for a long time. The drool that came from his mouth became a river that was full of foam that they called Expectation. He would be stuck there until Ragnarok came.

The Kidnapping of Idun

As the keeper of the fruit that granted the gods their long youth, Idun was easily the most important goddess in Norse mythology. Though it is not known exactly what fruit was the fruit of youth, the most common explanation is that of an apple.

One time, Hoenir, Odin, and Loki were traveling on a journey that took them far beyond the walls of Asgard. They were passing through extremely desolate mountains that had little to no food. Eventually, they came to a herd of oxen, and in their hunger, they slaughtered one almost immediately so they could eat.

They built up a fire and placed the meat from the oxen on top. After a while, they realized it was not cooking. The longer they left it on the fire, the more worried they became. It seemed that it did not matter what they did; the meat was refusing to cook.

Suddenly, there was a voice that came from above. It was an eagle, much larger than any regular eagle, perched on a tree nearby. The eagle told them that it was he who was preventing their meat from cooking, using magic. He told them that he would allow it to cook if they allowed him to choose what parts he wanted first.

Reluctantly, they agreed. The eagle allowed the meat to cook and then went first at choosing what parts he wanted. To Loki, the eagle was stealing all of the best parts of the meat for himself. This angered Loki to the point where he grabbed the closest branch and lunged at the eagle, hoping to hit him. The eagle was fast enough to grab the branch with his talons and fly away, with Loki still hanging onto the other side.

Loki began to beg for him to release him. It turned out that this eagle was actually a giant in disguise, the giant Thjazi. He said he would not let him go until Loki agreed to bring Idun and her fruits of youth to him.

Loki agreed, and the eagle let him down back where the others were. He did not tell the others what he had promised to do, and went with them back to Asgard. After they had safely returned, Loki immediately went to Idun and told her that he had found a fruit that seemed even better than the fruit she was famous for, in a forest that was on the other side of the walls of Asgard. He told her she should bring her own fruit and compare the two to see which one was better.

Not thinking anything of it, she followed him beyond the walls. Once they reached the woods he was speaking of, Thjazi swooped down and captured her, flying her far away from Asgard to where he lived. It was called Thryheim, or Thunder-Home, and was located among the highest mountain peaks. There were towers of ice that stood menacingly above, staring down at the more fertile land below.

Soon after, the gods began to feel the effects of aging; their hair began to gray, and their skin began to wrinkle. The youthful energy they used to have just dwindled away. They came together to figure out where Idun had gone, and soon came to the conclusion that Loki had been the last one seen with her.

Angry, they turned on Loki and demanded to know what had happened. They threatened him with the worst pain he could imagine to make sure he told them the truth. He quickly told them everything, from how the eagle had made him promise to send her to him, to the eagle taking her the second she was in range.

Instead of being sympathetic to what had happened, they told him he had to rescue Idun himself. Otherwise, they would sentence him to death for what he had done.

Freya lent him hawk feathers that she owned, which would give him the ability to transform himself into a hawk. Given the new ability, he was able to immediately fly away to Jotunheim, where not only the giants lived, but also Thjazi.

When he flew up to Thrymheim, he found that Idun was alone. Thjazi had gone out to sea to fish for their dinner. While Thjazi was gone, Loki transformed Idun into a small nut and took off back towards Asgard, with Idun nestled in his talons.

However, Thjazi returned soon after. He quickly figured out what had happened and changed himself into his eagle form, furiously following Loki. Even once Loki was finally able to see the walls of Asgard, he was unable to relax. Thjazi was closing the gap between them quickly.

In Asgard, once they saw what was happening with Loki and Thjazi, they quickly built a fire along the border. Loki made it across the barrier with Thjazi just behind him. As soon as Loki had entered, the gods lit up the fire, which exploded extremely quickly. There was no time for Thjazi to turn around, so he ran right into the flames, burning him. He fell to the ground injured, and was killed by the gods for his actions shortly after.

Njord and Skadi's Marriage

The gods were celebrating their victory of defeating Thjazi, who had done nothing but caused them trouble. They were so happy to finally have their beloved Idun back safe after her kidnapping. However, their partying was unable to go on for long.

Someone came bursting into their halls, breaking the happiness that they had. It was Skadi, a giantess that just so happened to be Thjazi's daughter. She had brought with her all sorts of armor and weapons in order to avenge his death. However, the gods were not easily swayed by her anger.

Slowly, they managed to calm her down and convince her she would be better off not trying to kill them. She should accept reparations instead of jumping to the side of revenge. So, they wrote up three different reparations and immediately began to complete them.

First, Odin would take Thjazi's eyes and toss them into the night sky. There, they would become two, glittering stars. This way, Skadi would be able to see her father every single night in the sky.

Second, they had to make her laugh. They tried many different things, but nothing they tried could make her even smile. She had seemingly put up a wall that was impossible for them to penetrate. However, they gave the reigns to Loki, who was able to think of something that was bound to make her laugh.

He found a rope and tied one end around a goat. The other end, he tied around his testicles. Then, he proceeded to play tug of war with the goat, trying to outmatch a much stronger animal. Both the goat and Loki tried their best, but in the end, Loki ended up falling over into Skadi's lap. At last, they were able to produce a chuckle out of her mouth.

Third, they were going to allow Skadi to choose one of the gods to marry. However, she was not going to be able to choose freely. They were only going to allow her to see the legs and feet of each god, and she needed to choose solely based on that.

All of the gods lined up, with everything hidden except for their legs and shoes. Carefully, Skadi studied each leg and foot, hoping she could figure out which one she truly wanted. She was hoping to get lucky and choose Baldur, the one god she had a crush on. She ended up choosing the legs and shoes that she believed to be the finest.

Instead of Baldur, she chose Njord, who was a god of the sea.

They had a beautiful and magnificent wedding. After the wedding, they had to decide where they would live together. Njord lived in a place called Noatun, which was a warm, sunny place on the beach. However, Skadi lived in Thrymheim, which was the place of her father that was high in the mountains and full of cold and snow.

Instead of choosing right away, they decided to test out both and see which one they could both stand. First, they went to Thrymheim and spent nine nights there. Once they were done and on their way down the mountain, Njord spoke of his dislikes. He absolutely hated the cold and was even more upset about the howling of the wolves that kept him up at night. He missed the swan music he was accustomed to back home.

Next, they went to Noatun and spent nine nights there. Skadi felt a similar hatred to the beach that Njord had to the snow. She told him the cries from the seabirds had been so unbelievably hard on her ears that she could not fall asleep any of the nights they were there.

Instead of forcing one to stay where they did not want to, they chose to instead part ways, each going home to their favorite place. Their marriage ended soon after.

The Creation of Thor's Hammer

Loki decided one day that he was bored. To satiate his mood, he decided to go to Thor's wife, Sif, and shave all of her hair off.

When Thor found out, he was understandably furious. He went to Loki and threatened to break each and every bone in his body. As usual, Loki begged Thor to spare him and said he would go down to Svartalfheim and see if the dwarves could create Sif brand new hair. Thor agreed to it, especially after Loki promised the hair would be even more beautiful than her original hair.

Loki went down to Svartalfheim and met with the sons of the dwarf Ivaldi. Once they heard what they needed to do, they crafted the new hair for Sif. However, they did not stop there. They also created Skidbladnir, which was considered the best of all ships. It would always have a favorable wind no matter what direction it went, and was able to fold up so small it could be be placed in a pocket. Also, they created Gungnir, which would become the deadliest spear to ever be made.

Even though they had created what he needed, Loki did not want to leave. He wanted to stay in the caves and do more reckless things away from the gaze of the gods. The first thing he did was go to Brokkr and Sindri, who were two brothers, and taunted them. He told them he knew the brothers could never create something as magical as the three creations the Ivaldi brothers had made. He went a step further and said he would bet his head that they were lacking in that ability.

Brokkr and Sindri accepted the wager and immediately went to work. However, as they went to work, Loki transformed into a fly, sat on Sindri's hand, and stung it. Later, when they were done, Sindri pulled the creation he had been working on out of the fire to reveal Gullinbursti, which was a living boar that had golden hair. The boar produced light when it was dark and was able to run faster than any horse. It could even run through the water and the air.

Excited by his work, Sindri cast more gold into the fire while Brokkr worked on the bellows. Loki went to Brokkr and stung him on the neck. Soon after, Sindri pulled out the gold he had put in the fire to reveal Draupnir, an absolutely beautiful ring. This ring was able to produce eight golden rings every ninth night, making it truly extraordinary.

Sindri moved on to iron and put that in the fire. He informed Brokkr that they needed to be absolutely meticulous with the next creation. They could not make a single mistake, or it would be worse than if they had messed up on the previous creations. Hearing of their plan, Loki quickly went to Brokkr's eyelid and stung it, completely blocking his view from that eye.
Sindri crafted a hammer that was of the best quality in the universe. This hammer would never be able to miss its mark and could even boomerang back to the owner after it was thrown. For all of its great abilities, there was a downfall: the handle was rather short.

He was upset at the flaw, but that did not mean it was unusable. He gave it the name Mjolnir, meaning Lightning. Knowing the amazing worth of everything they had created, they went to Asgard to get the money they believed they were due.

Loki went back to Asgard with all of the creations in tow; he provided Thor with the hair he had promised for Sif, and the hammer Mjolnir. He gave Odin the magnificent ring Draupnir, and the amazing spear Gungnir. He even provided Freyr with Skidbladnir and Gullinbursti.

The gods were incredibly grateful for everything Loki had gifted them. They were especially happy with Mjolnir, which they believed would aid them greatly in the future. However, they also decided that the dwarves were due Loki's head. They believed that Brokkr and Sindri's creations were more magnificent than the things the other brothers had made.

As the dwarves went up to Loki with their knives at the ready, he decided to point out that he had only promised them his head, not his neck. They consented to only sewing Loki's mouth shut and not chopping his head off, before going back to their forge.

Fishing for Jormungand

At one time, the gods decided to have a lavish and large feast with the two giants Aegir and Ran. They were always very hospitable and friendly to the gods, which was rare among giants. The giants said they would be willing to host the feast if the gods were able to find a kettle that would be large enough to brew mead for every single person that was invited to the banquet.

The gods knew where they would be able to find one, but they also knew it would not be easy to obtain. The kettle belonged to Hymir, who was a giant that did not get along with the gods at all.

Thor, who was always considered the strongest and bravest of the gods, volunteered to get the cauldron from Hymir. He was the most accustomed to dealing with giants, as he was usually sent to stop them when they tried to invade.

When Thor arrived at Hymir's house, Hymir went and killed three bulls to provide enough food for the both of them during the entirety of Thor's stay. Thor, however, had an incredibly high appetite and ate two of them during the first night of his stay. Hymir was very angry and stated they would both be going fishing in the morning for more food.

Hymir told Thor to go and get bait for the fish, bright and early in the morning. Not knowing exactly what to do, Thor went to

Hymir's fields and killed his largest bull, declaring he would use the head as bait.

Hymir's anger was only getting worse with every bad decision Thor made, but he did not say anything. He truly hoped Thor's strength would come in handy when they were able to go fishing.

They both went into a boat and began to row out into the water. Thor was at the stern of the boat. They first went Hymir's regular fishing spot. Quickly, Hymir managed to pull in two whales, much to his delight. However, Thor started to row the boat further from land, which began to make Hymir afraid.

Hymir knew the further they went from land, the more likely they would run into Jormungand, who was lurking beneath the surface of the water. However, Thor was Jormungand's oldest enemy, and he refused to turn back when he was so close.

Finally, Thor stopped rowing and tossed his line into the water. There was a period of absolute silence, which was only causing even more panic in Hymir. Suddenly, there was a huge tug on the line.

Thor began to reel the line back furiously. There was a rumbling that shook the boat violently and caused the waves to grow in size. Hymir knew what was happening, and it made his face turn completely pale.

Thor's feet were planted firmly on the boat's bottom, causing it to splinter. After what seemed like forever, Jormungand's head finally came above the water, his mouth dripping with venom. Thor grabbed his hammer as he came above the water.

Hymir completely panicked at seeing Jormungand and sliced the fishing line that was connected to him. As soon as Jormungand felt the line break, he sunk back into the sea, going back to his hiding place.

Enraged, Thor pushed Hymir overboard, allowing him to be taken by Hymir. Now alone, Thor made his way back to the land with the two whales that Hymir had caught over his shoulders. He picked up the cauldron the gods had been looking for, and made his way back home to Asgard.

Thor the Cross-Dresser

There was one morning where Thor woke up to see that his hammer, Mjolnir, was missing. Without his hammer, Asgard was vulnerable to attacks made by the giants. He searched absolutely everywhere for it, but he could not find it anywhere.

Freya owned falcon feathers, giving the wearer the ability to transform into a falcon. She allowed Thor and Loki to borrow them so they could look for the hammer much more easily.

After searching for it, Loki finally concluded that giants had most likely stolen the hammer. With this new information, he went to Jotunheim, the world of the giants.

When he got there, he transformed back into his regular god form. He walked up to Thrym, who was the chief of the giants and asked him some questions about the hammer. Thrym told him he had been the one to take it and that it was buried eight miles underground. He also said he refused to return it to the people of Asgard until Freya would marry him.

Loki returned to Asgard and told them of Thrym's demand. Understandably, the gods were furious with the demand, most of all, Freya. They immediately got to talking in a council meeting, trying to figure out what they should do about the situation. Heimdall was the first to put forth a potential solution.

He said they should have Thor disguise himself as Freya and go to Jotunheim to steal the hammer back himself. He would be able to enter Jotunheim easily while being disguised, and would be able to enact his vengeance on those who stole his hammer.

Thor was outraged at the idea, stating it was completely unmanly and dishonorable to do such a thing. He was convinced all of the people in Asgard would mock him for the rest of his life if he did something like that. Loki decided to point out the little fact that if Thor refused, Asgard would more than likely end up being ruled by the giants in the near future. This was the only thing that changed Thor's mind.

In order to send Thor there in perfect disguise, they had to create the perfect wedding dress for the occasion. The gods made sure every single detail was perfect on the dress, making it fit for a queen. Once it was complete, Thor put it on. The veil that was built into the dress perfectly covered his face. Loki decided he would go with Thor under the guise of being his maid-servant.

They traveled to Jotunheim on Thor's goat-driven chariot. When they arrived, Thrym was there waiting. He was absolutely ecstatic that the gods had sent Freya to him and believed he had finally received the prize he was due.

However, that night at dinner, the pair found themselves in the heart of danger. Without thinking of the consequences, Thor ate eight salmon, a full oven, and all of the dainties that had been made specifically for the women. On top of that, he also swallowed many, many barrels of mead during the night. His insatiable appetite had gotten him into trouble.

Thrym was suspicious at the amount of food being shoved into his new bride's mouth. He said he had never seen any woman consume so much food in his entire life. Loki, however, was a quick thinker and told him that Freya was simply so overcome with love for Thrym that she had not eaten anything during the course of the week.

He accepted this answer and became overwhelmed with the desire to kiss Freya. He went to her and pulled back the veil just enough to see Thor's eyes glaring back at him. They were not the soft eyes he had expected, and he quickly stated that they were "frightfully piercing."

Once again, Loki came to the rescue and told him that just as Freya had trouble eating throughout the last week, she had also been completely unable to sleep. She was just so overcome with the desire to finally be with Thrym that she had been unable to function properly. Thrym was once again accepting of this answer.

Soon after dinner, the wedding ceremony began. Thrym followed the usual customs and went to get the hammer to make their union official. He placed the hammer in his bride's lap, not knowing what would happen soon after.

Thor wasted no time, grabbed the hammer, and killed Thrym. Then, he killed all of the guests and returned to Asgard. He made sure to quickly change back into his favorite clothes as soon as he returned.

The Duel Between Thor and Hrungnir

Hrungnir was always seen as the most fearsome and mightiest of the giants. However, one day, he was visited by Odin in his home within Jotunheim. At first, he did not know exactly who he was. He outwardly said he wondered who had a horse that could both ride in water and through the air.

Odin decided he would bet his own head that the horse he owned would be able to outrun every horse in Jotunheim. Hrungnir was offended by the accusation and accepted his bet immediately. To start with, he decided to mount his own horse, whose name was Gullfaxi.

They took off and raced through steams, over rocky hills that were incredibly steep, and through the thickest woods, dodging trees the whole time. Without realizing what had happened, he found himself entering the gates of Asgard. He had still not caught up with Odin and his horse, Sleipnir.

The gods were quite happy and invited Hrungnir to join them in their drinking. He gladly accepted and soon became drunk and belligerent. Hrungnir started bragging about how he would kill every god except for Sif and Freya. He would then carry both of them back to Jotunheim to be with him. Freya continued to give him more mead, regardless of what he was saying.

Not long after, he yelled out, declaring that he would drink the ale in everyone else's cups, not letting them have any more. Soon, however, the gods grew incredibly tired of his anger and had someone go and fetch Thor.

When Thor came back and saw what was happening, he was ready to kill Hrungnir, where he stood. Instead, Hrungnir told Thor that he was a complete coward for wanting to kill someone who was completely unarmed. Then, he told him that he would rather challenge him to a duel. If Thor accepted, he would be held in a much higher regard than before.

The arranged time for the duel came, and Hrungnir went to a field near Jotunheim. He was decked out with stone armor, a stone shield, and had a whetstone, which was always his go-to weapon of choice. He brandished it high above his head. Lightning and thunder appeared above him, which signaled the appearance of Thor.

Thor quickly engaged in the duel. He threw his hammer directly at Hrungnir while Hrungnir through his whetstone at Thor. The whetstone smacked Thor directly in the head, and shattered into thousands of little pieces. This was said to be the origin of all the flint that was on earth in Midgard.

The hammer, however, made contact with Hrungnir's head and shattered his head into many pieces, killing him instantly.

There was still a small piece of the whetstone stuck in Thor's forehead. Unable to remove it himself, he went in search of Groa, a sorceress. When he found her, she sang many spells at the stone in order to remove it from his head. Soon, he felt the stone begin to move, and he started telling Groa all sorts of things to encourage her to keep going.

One of the things he told her was that he had actually met her husband, who was lost, and that he was going to return home very soon. This made Groa become so overwhelmed with emotion that she completely forgot what chants she was singing.

She was unable to continue the removal of the stone, which meant Thor would be stuck with it in his head until his eventual demise during Ragnarok.

The Tale of Utgarda-Loki

Thor and Loki were once traveling in Thor's chariot that was drawn by goats, very far from Asgard. They stopped during the night and were allowed to stay in the home of a farming family.

To repay them for allowing the two to stay the night, Thor said he would gladly make his goats their dinner that night. He knew that he would be able to bring them back to life later on, so it would not cause any harm to offer them for the meal.

Once the meal was done, Thor had their hosts lay the hides from his goats on the floor. Thor instructed them to lay the bones on top of the hides once all the meat had been taken.

The farmer had two young children, a son, and daughter. The son's name was Thjalfi, and the daughter's name was Roskva. Even though Thor had told them they needed to put the bones back onto the hide intact, Thjalfi had broken one of the bones and sucked out all of the marrow. When he put the bone back onto the hide he made it look like it had not been broken.

In the morning, Thor prepared the bones and hides before bringing the goats back to life. However, instead of them coming perfectly back to life, one of the goats now had a limp hind leg. It did not take long for Thor to figure out exactly what had happened.

He turned to the family and was completely furious at what they had done. He was nearly on the edge of killing all of them for their actions. The farmer was terrified for his family and ended up offering his two children to be Thor's servants. This made Thor change his mind about killing them. He accepted their offer, and they took the children with them on foot, leaving the two goats behind.

Their journey was leading them to Jotunheim. It was not easy, especially with two children with them. They traveled through a very thick forest and crossed an entire ocean to get to their destination.

As night was drawing close, they found themselves just outside of a huge hall. They investigated and found nobody inside, making it the ideal place to spend the night.

In the middle of the night, they were rudely awoken by a great earthquake. They all ran outside to see where the earthquake came from, and came face to face with a giant. The giant was fast asleep on the ground, and it was his snoring that was causing the earthquake that awoke them.

As Thor had an incredible hatred for giants, he knew he had to kill the giant. He prepared to kill the giant with his hammer but was not expecting the giant to wake up before he could. The giant was surprisingly happy to see Thor and all of his companions with him.

He told them his name was Skrymir, which meant Boaster, and let them know that he already knew who they were. He picked up his glove, which just happened to be the hall where they had slept the night before, and put it back on. He told them he would be happy to join them on their journey. Thor agreed that he could join them, and they continued their journey.

They took shelter beneath a great oak tree the next night. Skrymir had been the one to carry all of their things in his bag, and left it to Thor to open once he fell asleep. However, Thor was not able to untie all of the knots that were holding the bag shut. This made Thor grow irrationally angry to the point where he threw his hammer at the giant's head, hoping it might actually kill him.

Instead of it killing him, however, he awoke and asked them if something light like a leaf had hit him on the head.

It did not take long for Thor to become annoyed once again. Skrymir began to snore incredibly loud to the point where Thor was unable to sleep properly. Once again, he attempted to smite the giant and kill him. And, just like before, the giant woke up and asked, this time, if an acorn had awoken him by falling on his head.

Right before dawn came, Thor decided he would try one last time to kill Skrymir. Just as before, the giant woke up, asking if birds had roosted above him, pushing the dirt from the branches onto his face.

After Thor's final failed attempt, Skrymir decided to leave them to continue their journey on their own. Thor and the others continued on towards their final goal, which was a castle called Utgard. In the middle of the day, they were finally able to reach the castle. However, the gates to the castle were locked when they arrived.

There was no one there who was able to open the gate for them. However, they were able to find a large enough gap between the bars where they could fit through. Inside the castle, they found themselves in a hall where there were men who were eating and drinking.

Utgarda-Loki was the king of the castle and was one of the men who were eating. When he saw Thor and the others, he knew exactly who they were. He wasted no time in taunting them about their smaller size.

Loki, in an attempt to save his dignity, told the giants that no one in the hall could eat food faster than he could. Utgarda-Loki decided to challenge him to prove this bold claim. He would enter an eating contest with Logi, one of the other men in the hall.

A large trough of meat was placed in between them. They were sat on either end, and their goal was to be the first to make it to the middle. After they began, it did not take them long to both meet in the middle at the same time. However, it soon became apparent who the true winner was. Loki had eaten all the meat off of the bones. Logi, however, had eaten the meat, bones, and the trough that was holding the meat.

Next, Thjalfi came forward and said he was a very fast runner and said he would race anyone in the castle. Hugi was asked to race him on a track outside. When Hugi made it all the way around the track, he realized that Thjalfi was still pretty far back, so he doubled back to meet up with him. They raced two more times, Thjalfi winning easily every time.

Thor then decided he would challenge someone in the castle to a drinking contest. He did not have very much skill when it came to drinking. Utgarda-Loki had a servant bring him one of the horns that his men used to drink from. He told Thor that the best drinkers could finish it in one gulp, and the fair drinkers could finish it in two. However, no one who was impressive would finish it in three or more.

Thor started to drink as fast as he could. When he paused to catch his breath, he realized that barely any of the drink was gone. He tried much harder with the second gulp, but he still was unable to last long enough to finish the drink. He tried once more, but even then, he could not finish it and gave up.

Utgarda-Loki then gave Thor the challenge of lifting his cat from the floor. As much as he tried, it was impossible for him to do.

In his annoyance, Thor demanded to challenge someone to wrestle him. Utgarda-Loki had him wrestle an older woman named Elli, one of his servants. It proved impossible yet again for Thor to complete this contest.

Utgarda-Loki then decided to put an end to the contests, and had everyone spend the night in the castle.

The next morning, they got ready to leave, and Utgarda-Loki led them out of the castle. He then told them what had actually happened. He was in fact, Skrymir. All of the blows Thor had tried to kill him with had missed and created valleys in the mountainside. The ties on the bag were impossible to release because they were made from iron.

He also told him that Loki did a phenomenal job eating the meat, but his opponent was actually fire itself. Thjalfi also did a great job, but no one would be able to outrun thought. The horn that Thor drank from was connected to the sea, which is what made it so difficult to drink. His cat was the Midgard serpent, which Thor had successfully raised out of the ocean. Finally, the old woman he had wrestled was, in fact, old age, which always took a long time to fall.

Utgarda-Loki then warned them that they should never return.

Thor was angry and decided this was the time where he would finally kill the giant. He grasped his hammer and turned to kill him, but the giant had disappeared. In fact, the castle had disappeared also! All that remained was a wide-open landscape. Thor and Loki returned to Asgard, feeling defeated.

Conclusion

Thank you for making it through to the end of *Norse Mythology*! I hope that you thoroughly enjoyed learning about the different gods, goddesses, heroes, monsters, and famous Norse mythology stories!

The Germanic people had a vibrant and interesting religion that they followed. Everything was not perfect on earth; even their gods were not perfect. Gods like Odin had numerous faults, but he also stood strong when the people needed him the most.

Other gods, such as Loki, may have been a little more hated than others, but still played an important part in this religion. Every god, dwarf, giant, and elf was important in the grand scheme of the religion, especially when it came to the end during Ragnarok.

Many of the gods that come from Norse mythology are still talked about today. Throughout popular culture, there are many mentions of the different gods in various capacities. For example, many of today's movie superheroes are based on gods from Norse mythology. Though their stories may be quite different from the original mythology, you should now have a good understanding of where these characters originated from!

Finally, if you're interested in learning more about mythology, keep an eye out for my other books. In addition to Norse mythology, I have books available on Greek, Egyptian, and Celtic mythology!

Thanks again for choosing this book, I hope you enjoyed it!

CPSIA information can be obtained
at www.ICGtesting.com
Printed in the USA
BVHW091531201221
624502BV00009B/628